Stories My Father Told Me

James Lockett Malony

FRONT PORCH HISTORY

2012

About the Author
Major General Harry Malony was a veteran of over 40 years in the U.S. Army in both command and staff responsibility. He was a graduate of West Point, Class of 1912, and served in the Mexican Border Campaign as well as in the Panama Canal as it was under construction. He was armament consultant to the French Air Force in WWI, Infantry Division Commander in WWII, Supervisor of the Greek Great Free Elections, and various diplomatic missions, postwar. Harry Malony was a born raconteur with a lighthearted view of the world which he shared with his friends and associates and which he passed along in his stories to me.

About the Son of the Author
James Lockett Malony is a graduate of West Point 1945, and is currently the latest member of a line of graduates starting in 1854 plus one Naval Commodore in 1807, which was the highest Naval rank at the time. James served as an Infantry Unit Commander in 1945 Philippines and Japan before returning to the United States and starting his own consulting company, serving U.S. Clients in Europe, West Africa, South America and Russia. He also continued to serve the U.S. government in providing training services.

Copyright 2012 James L. Malony
ISBN-13: 978-0-9855969-1-0

Contents

Introduction	vi
Foreword	vii
I Stories My Father Told Me	1
El Toro	2
The Pilot's Tale	11
Tropical Democracy	18
The Championship	33
Vive Le France	41
Pecans	45
Innocence Rewarded	49
Lost Over	55
Gangster	63
Tramp	65
The Irish Dilemma	68
Portrait of a Bretonne	73
"Charlie"	80
The White Bird	84

The *Apache*	87
The Guard Post	90
Uncivil War	92
Erin Go Braugh!	93
Mounted Murder	95
The Refined One	101
The Half Crown Story	104
One World	106
You Can Never Hurt A Drunk	108
The Faith Healer	111
Tragedy in New England	113
Allies	115
Mussoorie	120
II Our Blessed Country	123
Introduction	124
Sinking Of The *Chesapeake* (1807)	125
John Malony's Letter To The Hon. Ryland Fletcher (1862)	127
John Malony's Letter To Provost At Georgetown College (1864)	131
Unsung Hero	133
A Boy's Letter to His Mother (1943)	135
Leander's Story (1944)	138

Stephen Ross's Story (1945)	139
War Crimes (1946)	141

III Postscript 143

Poems My Father Wrote	144
Ancient Wisdom	150
Colonel Fatass	151
Ancestors	152

Introduction

Stories My Father Told Me

When you are a sixth generation military descendent such as I one collects all manner of records, heirlooms, narratives and stories; some of these are in family records (Lockett, Malony, and Huson volumes); others became parts of historical accounts. From mounds of data come a group of personal stories, which reflect not only a soldier's sense of humor, but also an insight into the social and physical environment of the times.

My father, Maj. Gen. H.J. Malony, was a poet and a grand storyteller throughout his 82 years as a military officer and soldier-diplomat. Hence the bulk of the stories are his. I have included a few of his philosophical writings also for good measure.

My own stories are in a separate volume, *Kaleidoscope*, but I like these just as well!

Foreword

Everyone has stories, but I consider Jim Malony to be the best story teller I have ever met. In this book, his father's stories come to life. Jim dutifully collected these stories over the years and is now able to present them in this historic and thrilling book. This book is a companion to Jim's stories published in *Kaleidoscope*. I read his father's stories years ago and persuaded Jim to publish and share them with the world.

    I never met his father, Major General Harry J. Malony, West Point class of 1912. However, after reading his stories, I feel like I know him. Jim certainly inherited the art of telling stories from his dad, as you will testify to at the end. As a Division Commander in WWII, Major General Harry Malony gives you detailed stories about life in combat. His unique perspective gives you the behind the scenes view of what he saw and heard. His stories piece together a quilt, that when complete, gives you a much richer appreciation of history.

    With the help of a world class editor and friend of many West Pointers, Remy Benoit, Jim's father's stories are finally compiled and published in honor of his father.

    Like Jim Malony, his father had a wealth of experiences—many more than most of us.

    I consider Jim a dear friend. The bonds of being fellow West Pointers (Class of 1945 and Class of 1968) tie us together for life as brothers; we have grown and strengthened that bond in the time we spend together whether on the golf course or in doing business.

    It is an honor to have helped Jim to get this book to press. Enjoy it as I did.

—Chuck Giasson, Colonel Ret. U.S. Army
West Point Class of 1968

EDITOR'S NOTE: These stories are representative of oral history. They are representative of their times and do not represent the beliefs of the editor, publisher, or any one other than their respective authors.

Major General Harry J. Malony, Commanding General 94th Inf Div, Sept 15 1942–May 21, 1945 with his aide.

Signing of the Bases for "Battleship" Treaty with Great Britain in the Caribbean in the early 1940s. My dad is at the end of the table.

Part I
Stories My Father Told Me

El Toro

> I suggest that in order to really enjoy this story, the reader should try to envision the Bull Fight as described—this is a very funny story told by my father who was Officer of the Day in the Army stationed in Panama when the Bull Fight occurred. Why a riot at the stadium did not occur is beyond my belief.

El Toro

The night was quiet and from the stables off in the distance came those noises which mere soldier that I am, in common with all the Garrison, I had begun to love: horses stamping and eating, the rattle of halter chains in the evening's quiet, The slow walk of the sentry's horse down the road behind the stable area.

All of a sudden, I was filled with inspiration. "Major," I said, "Let's take our friends down town and watch the dance." The Major is not keen about dancing, but loves to watch.

The offer of a car was quickly accepted, and shortly we were in our favorite resting place on the porch of the Hotel Howard. The strains of a popular Fox Trot filtered through to us, and someone had produced a guaranteed pre-war drink.

"You told us the other night," I began hopefully, "that you had seen the two most sporting events ever held. One was a prizefight.[1] What was the other?" The Major uncrossed his knees, and slid back in his chair and settled himself comfortably.

"Well," he said, "I expected this some day. I like to recall it.

"With the great influx into Panama, of workmen, soldiers—and soldiers back in 1910 were all young, mostly unmarried—it was no more than natural that all kinds of athletics and sports should be great drawing cards. As a matter of fact, they were worked overtime. Our Panamanian friends found them very interesting and, of course, adopted all American sporting terms in a highly creditable fashion.

---

[1] The story of the prizefight is told below as "The Championship"

"We were discussing the athletic situation one night in the Hotel Centrale. The discussion was fast taking on the appearance of one sort of sporting event, an endurance contest, for the table was covered with bottles. We were holding forth with some of our sportiest and wealthiest Panamanian friends. The discussion had centered around the terrific energy of the Americans in things physical. A prizefight was scheduled for the coming week; a swimming competition was billed for Colon; and diverse other smaller meets were to take place at other places on the Zone.

"Our friends were agreed that all these were fine in their own peculiar places, but they argued, 'Why not be broadminded about sports in general? Why not concede that there were other sports much esteemed by other nations capable of being favorably compared with the best American ones?

"'For instances, take a bullfight. Best beloved of all Spanish-speaking people. Colorful. Gorgeous. The *picadores* on blindfolded horses, riding to danger, very possibly to death; the *banderilleros* facing the charge of the maddened bull as calmly as you would order a drink; the matador, greatest of all gladiators of the bull ring, whose unerring sword finally brought the maddened bull's last charge to an abrupt end.'

"We were in a broadminded mood. Many visits by the waiter had brought us to this pass. Nothing seemed impossible, or of much trouble. Why not bring a bullfight to Panama? We furnished the idea. Let our Spanish friends carry it out. *¡La Verdad! ¡Criado, otro trago! ¡Pase la botella!* You know how it is. Much enthusiasm: no action anticipated, nor expected.

"Considerable action did start from our suggestion though. It developed that there was quite a troupe, or circus, or whatever you call a complete outfit of bullfighter down in Peru; and that although the shows they were putting on were nothing short of remarkable, they were having their financial troubles. They could be induced to come up. A meeting was held and the requisite money was pledged the following day. Everyone knew that with a little American advertising all could be made well.

"Even if the bull fighters weren't up to old world standards, it was certain that there would be no harm done, since not more than one American out of a hundred had ever seen a real *corrida de toros*.

"One thing led to another. Arrangements were quickly made. The Government of Panama got its guarantee of one quarter; one eighth went to the Church; another to the Department of Education; the police and firemen and various other municipal officers accounted for another; and our promoters seemed content with what was left, which after all was said and done, seemed to consist mainly of prestige.

"For the next three weeks billboards, bulletin boards, and the Commission eating-houses were adorned with posters notifying the public of the resurrection in Panama of the finest of Spanish sports. In the Commission eating-houses, the ordinary place to locate the poster was over the table containing the tray of rum and quinine. The Chief seemed to feel that the local flavor of one might enhance that of the other.

"By a most trying chain of circumstances, the week of the *corrida*, I was doing duty as Provost Marshal of Panama City. You may see nothing particularly noteworthy in that, but believe it or not, such a tour of duty in those days when Panama was wide open was likely to be equivalent of a night patrol on the Western Front.

"Our particular battlefront was in the Cocoa Grove District. If you can picture a couple of thousand sailors, and a like number of soldiers and canal workers just paid for the month, and congregated in an area of, say ten acres of disreputable buildings, just itching for someone to start something, you may get some inkling of what a busy night in the Cocoa Grove District could produce.

"Now, this duty changed my whole reaction to the bullfight. I anticipated that the soldiers and sailors might find things a bit slow. I knew that if they did, by the same token, they would start something. If this occurred, I knew that I was in for a bad time as my most important duty as Provost Marshal was to preserve order among the troops while in the City. Well, I was certain to be among the troops and they were certain to be in the City.

"Let's see. Where was I? When I discovered that I was to be in charge so to speak, during the bullfight, I made the most elaborate preparations I could think of. I decided to put my Sergeant on the *entrada* with the ticket taker. He was to watch the incoming crowd as to uniforms, and to spot any semblance of concerted action contrary to good order. The remainder of my small group I deployed in pairs throughout the grandstand. It was a certainty that all Americans would be there and not in *El Sol* (the bleachers).

"As for myself, I went up to the box of the Chief of Police where I could observe the crowd entering and where my view of the American section of the grandstand was unimpeded.

"You should have seen the crowd entering. The van guard was mostly white, with here and there a group of East Indians and Chinese. Jamaicans, Barbadians, Hondurans, San Bias Indians, copper colored Caribs. These all took their places in *El Sol*. The Indians removed the shoes from their aching feet. All waited stolidly.

"Then the Europeans began to arrive. The *Presidente* and the Chief of Police both came in new automobiles of an expensive American make. Their cars were filled with the feminine members of their respective *ménages*, all well groomed and gowned in the latest from Paris. These two cars were closely followed by a third and fourth filled to overflowing with French and Spanish ladies from the Cocoa Grove District. They quite outshone their predecessors in the matter of dress.

"Taking advantage of the police lines keeping the pathway clear for the *Presidente's* passage, they paraded toward the *entrada*. I can still see them in their high-heeled shoes and plumed hats, strutting through the ankle deep dust at the entrance of the bullring, heedless of the remarks of admiring male friends whose ranks marked their line of march.

"After them, the deluge: hosts of American soldiers and sailors, all the Legation people, canal workers from hard rock men to superintendents, and natives. Some I recognized from the upper Bayano.

"They wore wide, hand-woven straw hats, their clothes were once white, and all were barefooted. It was a gala day. A perfect Babel came up to me. I could hear Chinese, Portuguese, French, Spanish, Italian and English conversations. It was really quite extraordinary—a Panamanian sporting event—a veritable international affair.

"The program listed a formidable array of bull fighting talent. The principal actor in the piece was to be *El Chico*, the *matador*. The best Peru had to offer. Recently arrived from Spain he had won instant acclaim in South America.

"Well, we had the regular parade. You know the kind. The *picadors* on their sorry doomed horses; the *banderilleros* with their brilliant cloaks; numbers of attendants, all headed by the famous *El Chico*. A more villainous looking Spaniard you would have had a long day's march to find. In the conventional knee breeches and the broad hat, his *coleta* (pig tail) carefully coiled beneath it, he presented a beetle browed, sun baked face to the audience. To me he looked more like the bull than the bull did.

"This sight seemed to prove too much for the assemblage of soldiers and sailors and one section surrounding a Spanish-speaking Corporal immediately started a cheer for the bull. ¡*El toro!* they yelled, ¡*Viva el toro!*. This was quickly taken up by the entire grandstand. A rollicking chorus ¡*Viva el toro!* started *El Sol* shrieking a rebuttal in seven languages.

"The procession stopped beneath the box of the *Presidente*, which was directly beneath my own. The *matador* after an ardent speech, tossed his hat up to the *Presidente's* sister and she threw him a rose. The grandstand cheered lustily. The party was ready to proceed.

"Well, the fight started in the regular fashion, except that the first bull refused to participate in it. He was quite befuddled at all this uncalled for attention. The *banderilleros* twisted his tail and drove him sulking along, striking him contemptuously with their cloaks. It was very hot and they were short of temper. They joined with the spectators in the cry for another bull.

"Having seen bullfights before, I had not forgotten my soldiers and sailors. A messenger sent to gather reports from my patrols found everything quiet, and the Sergeant coming along to report confirmed this somewhat doubtfully by stating that in his opinion it was 'too damn quiet.' He had noticed nothing out of the way, but remarked that there was great consumption of beer among the inhabitants of the grandstand. I, too, had noticed that. The Balboa-Best-Beer-Brewed people had clothed a score of pretty girls in bullfighters costumes and had sent them through the stand selling beer. From where I was sitting I could see them exchanging badinage with groups of soldiers and sailors and as I looked along the rows of seats, I saw that practically every American in sight had a bottle of beer either in his hands or down between his feet on the floor.

"The second bull was introduced and he was made of sterner stuff. The horses had been omitted as a gracious gesture to the Americans who saw no fun in a horse gored. The *banderilleros* took him on fresh and ready for battle. It was very pretty. *Pase* after *pase* with the horns of the bull barely missing his man. The soldiers and sailors liked this. They applauded wildly and it was well worth their applause. Two pairs of brilliantly colored darts were neatly affixed in the bull's neck as he charged. This latter was evidently intended to annoy the natives in *El Sol*.

"This play continued for some time and finally a loud blare of trumpets marked the entrance of *El Chico*. He dedicated the kill to the *Alcalde* in time-honored fashion and marched toward the bull in a decidedly professional fashion. With his short cloak carelessly dangling in front of him, he enticed the bull to a charge. The bull promptly responded. The *matador* slid his coat sideways with the greatest dexterity and the bull passed directly under his arm. The horns didn't miss by an inch. Again—bolder this time.

"The bull was obviously tiring. The *matador* proceeded to get ready for the kill. He was working now to get him in the proper position for the fatal stroke. Suddenly he tautened. The bull was preparing to charge. Sword poised for the blow the *matador* was ready.

"*¡El toro! ¡El toro!* A frantic yell from three thousand soldiers and sailors was accompanied by a volley of beer bottles from the grandstand. I saw at least half a dozen hit the bull. One removed *El Chico's* hat with great celerity. Another came to rest against his ribs. My men were up and doing but *¿Que tal?* What could they do?

"Well, I was struck dumb with astonishment. I realized that I had really become quite interested in that bullfight and that my duties had been momentarily forgotten. I looked for the *matador*. There he was running frantically around the ring. A black object passed him also running, but in the opposite direction. It was the bull. Neither paid the other the slightest attention. Moving targets being harder to hit, firing was now being conducted individually. Showers of bottles fell just behind. The *matador* dodged a baker's dozen in his stride. The bull was the target for the left wing. His tail clapped down tight, he was looking for a way out. The *matador* disappeared through a niche to the right of the stand and as he did so a bottle splintered not three inches above his knuckles, whitened by the intensity of his grip on the timbered frame.

"Three thousand Americans rocked with unholy glee. My own ribs were sore from laughing.

"I hurried out to the stand, but the storm subsided as quickly as it arose. I closed the beer concession and sternly walked through the stands. All were serene as a summer's day.

"The spectators began yelling for another bull. There seemed to be a lot of scurrying round among the officials in the boxes down below. Things seemed to be at a standstill in the ring. From the labyrinths of *El Sol* there suddenly appeared a minor official in the dress of the bull-ring. In his hands he held a good American megaphone and in a hurried and uneasy fashion he announced that the next event would be a *novio*. This meant that the next bull could be taken on by any amateur bull-fighter who might present himself. Fortunately for me and my duties this announcement was made in excited salvos of Spanish.

"Before it could be translated freely throughout the stand my patrols were covering every entrance into the arena. They were effective and three thousand American soldiers and sailors, would-be bullfighters all, were finally cajoled back into their seats. The beer concession closed, they were unable to replenish their ammunition supply. Still they had made the best of a bad situation and sat back hopefully waiting for something to happen.

"They hadn't long to wait. A new bull had been prodded into the arena and was trotting restlessly up and down. Suddenly from the sun drenched benches of *El Sol* appeared a native figure, a veritable phantom. I had no difficulty in recognizing him as one of my Bayano River friends.

"The bull stopped his trotting and sniffed uneasily. Stock still he stood, with his head lowered. A hush swept over the throng. *El Sol* waited stolidly, but with painful attention. It was obvious that the man was drunk, terribly, suddenly drunk. His wide brimmed straw hat was stuck firmly on the back of his head. His shirt hanging well outside of his trousers, once white, but now a reddish gray, flopped against his thin legs as he walked. His broad bare feet wandered blindly through the dust and every now and then he would pitch forward, regain his balance in a few quick steps, pause and rock back and forth on his heels.

"During one of these intervals, he sighted the bull. A gleam of understanding came into his face. *¡Hola toro!* he yelled, and he walked squarely up to the astonished bull, and squinting his eyes in a painful effort at concentration, peered deep into the glassy orbs of that offended bull.

"From the *Presidente's* box down below, came an awed *¡Santa Maria!* From the grandstand came the soldiers' verdict expressed in a series of ecstatic 'poor damn fool.' *El Sol* waited with pleasant anticipation. A Panamanian doctor, carrying a black bag, started hastily through the rows of the grandstand down towards the arena. It was over in a second. The bull lowered his head and with a bellow of rage charged.

"I am certain that it couldn't occur again in a lifetime. The black-head rum consumed by that native finally had gained a victory. As the bull launched his charge, the backward sway of the drunken native was too much. No chance, nor any attempt to recover. A split second ahead of that charge our drunken friend fell backwards full length and lay still. I could see the soles of his feet, strangely white in the sunshine, silhouetted against the straw hats in *El Sol*.

"The lowered horns of the bull passed completely over the fallen native, barely grazing his supine figure. Not so the bull. The bull seemed to slow down and to walk with great precision straight up the shirt front of that grotesque figure. *¡Muerto!*, gasped the *Presidente* from beneath me. *Pobre Viejo*, muttered a feminine voice behind me. *¡Santa Maria!* was exploding like Chinese firecrackers all around me. "Another dead spig" was the verdict of our soldiery. *El Sol* cheered unrestrainedly.

"One of the professional bullfighters quickly ran in with his cape and enticed the bull away. Then another unexpected thing happened. That piece of grotesquerie lying limp as a grain sack there in the middle of the ring came suddenly to life. He jumped to his feet and swaying slowly backwards and forwards began to beat the dust from his soiled and crumpled clothes.

"Three thousand soldiers and sailors were on their feet as one and their cheers were a credit to their lungs. *El Sol* sputtered discontentedly. I saw the Cocoa Grove ladies clapping delightedly and yelling in robust French. The attendants quickly walked our actor away. Everyone applauded him.

"Now, these two events were enough for one day and they had quite exceeded my expectations. My ribs grew sore from laughter. The bull was still going strong. He seemed to be playing hide and seek with one of the *banderilleros* around the niches. *El Sol* settled back tranquilly for more. Battle, murder, and sudden death, they had come to see. They were thoroughly enjoying themselves.

"From the front seats of the grandstand there appeared another figure. I rubbed my eyes. A Jamaican, upon my word, clad in knee breeches, a red bandana around his waist, and in place of the conventional cape of the bullfighter, he carried a red parasol.

"He jumped down into the ring. Our soldiery leaned forward with intense interest. *El Sol* was excited, to judge from the movement of the straw hats. The Jamaican walked steadily towards the bull. The bull saw him now and trotted towards him ready to bestow upon his person a vicious welcome. The Jamaican took the parasol—which he had been carrying, opened and over his right shoulder—from its carrying place, extended it directly in front and rolled the handle rapidly between his hands. The bull promptly charged. Up went the parasol; the lithe Jamaican glided sideways—a beautiful *pase*.

"Once again the bull charged the parasol—another *pase*. Bolder now, the little Jamaican was doing the thing with true professional aplomb. The soldiery cheered lustily. The boxed applauded gravely. So did I. *El Sol* waited hopefully. This applause caught the Jamaican in the midst of another *pase*. It apparently pleased him for as the bull passed, he hooked the parasol over his shoulder and turned to bow. To the right, to the left, in front, he bowed.

"The bull somewhat tired from his previous efforts did not run so far in his charge. His last had been a little bit half-hearted anyway. He turned suddenly, caught sight of that bobbing parasol, lowered his head and launched a magnificent effort.

"Three thousand throats shrieked a warning. *El Sol* roused at last, howled with mirthful anticipation. The little Jamaican looked over his shoulder and sadly shortened his bow. He seemed to me to turn a ghastly greenish hue and then, man, he obeyed an impulse. With the bull a scant ten feet behind, he ran. No. He didn't run, he flew. Never have I seen a start at full throttle like that. Straight across the ring towards the nearest barrier. The bull was gaining slightly. He had not lowered his head and his eyes were fixed with determination on that hated parasol, which his unfortunate enemy had forgotten to discard. He was so close that he seemed to be breathing down the frightened Jamaican's neck.

" 'Run!'

"I never hoped to see such running. *El Sol* applauded wildly. Gales of laughter swept the grandstand.

"The attendant at the far end of the ring threw a gate open and shouted. A *banderillero* standing near a niche yelled and gestured. But that Jamaican had other things to think about. He knew where he was going. The nearest point in the five-foot barrier was his objective and he was doing his best.

"Eyes bulging, and ears actually seeming to bend forward in the strain of his effort, he gained the barrier, the bull within two feet. There was no pause in his stride.

"To this day I believe that that little black man simply ran up one side of the barrier and down the other. No, he didn't vault it—he ran it.

"You should have seen the grandstand. With tears of joy streaming, hoarse with laughter, the stand rocked. *El Sol* was bitter in its disappointment."

The Major chuckled at the reminiscence. "But what happened to the bull, Major?" I inquired. "Well, that was extraordinary, too. He ran through the gate the attendant had opened for the Jamaican and down the through the streets of the city. My soldiers and sailors got their chance as bullfighters after all. I finally had to pay a *vaquero* five dollars to round him up, and the United States still owes me the money."

The Pilot's Tale

> This is an account of a very brave Spanish Admiral, his unique end, and the innovative solution to a very complex diplomatic problem with the Spanish government.

The Pilot's Tale

Years ago I urged the General to write this story himself.

I liked it and it seemed to me to belong to history. He is gone now and perhaps there remains none other than myself who knows it. He always refused to write it, or anything else pertaining to himself or to his broad knowledge of Government matters unless his duty required him so to do.

He simply laughed me off and said that "He was not yet ready to lie down and chew his cud."

I doubt that there are many living who know that at the Spanish naval holocaust, which was Santiago, there were two Spanish Admirals in the battle. Cervera is the name connected with it here, and he deserved to be remembered, for in fine fashion he carried out a mission, which seems impossible even when we look back to the sea fighting conditions of 1898.

Why does he deserve this accolade? He sailed straight across the Atlantic Ocean, right into the center of operations of our vastly superior Navy, and made his Caribbean port without having been seen or reported by a single American ship. In doing this, he managed (with the help of the American newspapers which kept the eastern seaboard in nervous spasms of apprehension) to immobilize most of the U.S. Navy, which, in answer to frenzied appeals for help through both military and political channels, was given defensive missions to protect the principal Atlantic harbors and the East Coast shipping.

When the presence of the Spanish Fleet in the Caribbean was definitely established, the East Coast breathed a sigh of relief, and a portion of the U.S. Fleet on defensive missions was relieved forthwith, and our Fleet fighting strength was concentrated in the Caribbean.

The American public has long forgotten the enjoyably gossipy and exciting controversy of that day over the question of who was in command of the U.S. Fleet at the battle of Santiago—the famous Sampson-Schley Affair which is immaterial to this story—but it is probably the one thing, which keeps some knowledge of the fight living.

From the U.S. point of view, a fight in which there were only two casualties and no ships lost cannot be termed a desperate affair.

From the Spanish perspective, having one out of ten men in their ships' complements become casualties, and the entire Fleet destroyed, it was, indeed, significant. As a direct result, Spanish power disappeared forever from the New World.

Admiral Cervera and Admiral Villamil, the two Spanish Admirals of this story, were friends of long standing. In the many conferences called in Havana by the Captain General of Cuba, they had stood together in opposition to his fierce demands that they fight their outnumbered squadrons against the American Fleet for moral effect if for nothing else.

Both regarded such a course as sending to their deaths both ships and men, for no purpose tangible or intangible, except perhaps some advancement for their political superiors.

From Madrid, Cervera was ordered to seek a favorable time for a sortie and to go, anyway, regardless, when and if "the fall of the city became imminent."

Reluctantly they drew a plan for the sortie.

It was agreed that Villamil, in one of the ships of the light force which he commanded, should precede the *Maria Teresa*, Admiral Cervera's flagship; while others of the small craft should fan out, and with the leading torpedo boat try to create a diversion: the remainder to follow the heavy craft, for with their lighter armament they could not engage the American ships.

Indeed, they would be lucky if they were not sunk long before they could get within their own gun-range. Chances were that they would be unable to fire a single effective round.

It was Friday morning, July 1st, that the Spanish defenses were completely invested by our Army; and by that afternoon the Spanish authorities estimated that the fall of the city was "imminent."

Admiral Cervera ordered all his Captains, along with Admiral Villamil, to report to the *Maria Teresa* that night.

He gave them the estimate of the situation told to him by the Captain-General of the Island; that the city could not be held, and that in his opinion the time had arrived to put into effect the plans for the sortie with which all were familiar.

It must have been an awesome assembly. Cervera circulated a document, which all present who estimated that the fall of the City was imminent were asked to sign. Each knew that he was signing his own death-warrant—and more than that—knew that his Admiral agreed and that he, too, was signing his own.

Then they got down to the details. It would take some time to get back the crews, which had been sent to bolster up the land defenses. It would take time, too, to get up steam, but that could probably be done by Saturday afternoon.

Should it be a day or night sortie?

The channel, tortuous and difficult at best, was lighted up by the American searchlights to a point where even a small boat could not come out undiscovered. The chances of escape by day seemed better. Cervera decided to wait until morning.

And so, on the morning of Sunday, July 2nd, the Spanish Fleet steamed out of the harbor in careful formation and in dignified and pathetic bravery went to its death.

Now, sometime after the battle, General Leonard Wood had been appointed Governor General of Cuba; the Spanish Army had surrendered and General Wood had selected his staff and had assumed his new duties. Lieutenant McCoy had been one of those selected for the new Governor General's staff.

He was now at table in one of the recently reopened cafes in Havana, and musingly watching the camaraderie on display between the American and Spanish troops, mortal enemies of a few days before, but now drinking companions and friends.

He did not find it strange that members of the 29th Spanish Battalion, which had held the Blockhouse on San Juan Hill, and had caused the highest percentage of casualties among the Americans, were most sought after and were general favorites among the American soldiery. No one seemed to have much use for the Cubans for whom both sides thought they had been fighting.

At a table behind him a party was drinking solemnly; he noticed that a civilian was holding the floor. All at the table were leaning forward, intent on not missing a word of the speaker, and Lieutenant McCoy listened quietly at his table.

"I was with them," said the Voice in lilting Spanish. "I was in the first ship to emerge. I was with Admiral Villamil; for it was he who commanded. I was the harbor pilot who was to show the way to the heavy cruisers and the battleships, which were following after us.

"It was Sunday and we had been to early Mass in the darkness. It was not cold, but we shivered, and when the day came we knew that it was not the right kind of weather for a sortie. The air was clear and it was steamy hot. The water was flat and tranquil and as we moved toward that narrow harbor entrance, I could hear the wake of the *Maria Teresa* as it went swishing along the bordering cave-lined shores.

"It was deathly quiet.

"There was not a sound on board.

"But now I could see them out there waiting. Those gray painted ships of the Americans were moving, and the smoke roiled from their stacks so black and thick that it was hard to pick them up beneath the clouds of it.

"We left the green water of the harbor and made the turn to port to enter into the purple water of the sea. I knew that the Admiral had intended to drop me at the usual place for the pilot, but he was lost in wonderment at the array of American ships which he was observing through his glasses. Behind us, the *Maria Teresa* was blowing the bugle signal to open fire; we could hear every note of it, clear and proud.

"Then the jagged blow torch jets of pure flame stabbed through the black smoke clouds covering the American ships. They were firing. The Admiral turned calmly to me. 'They will take us under fire now, and I would advise you to jump overboard and swim ashore.'

"'*Gracias, Señor Almirante, pero,*' said I stupidly, 'I will stay here with you.'

"He made a motion with his hand, and turned his glasses again to the on-coming American ships. 'We cannot reach them. We will never get within our own gun range, but we may as well shoot for the benefit of the gun crews.'

"He turned to the bugler, but he never gave the order. It was then that the first American shell came aboard. It hit right beneath us as we stood there on that little bridge on the pygmy ship.

"It exploded and tore up the old wooden deck and made each tiny piece of it into a separate missile. The Admiral was hit and toppled over on me. I managed to hold him up and yelled for help, for it seemed that I was hit too and thought I was dying, but nothing had touched me.

"The Admiral called for a chair and had one, a wicker one, placed on the bridge and they tied him in it. He continued to command."

Silence as the man drank deeply of his wine, as did all his companions. The Voice resumed.

"No one took the wheel from me and I continued to steer, but when I looked at the Admiral I knew that he was going to die. He knew that I was watching him and made a little motion with his hand—like that, *Señor*—for me to continue at my job. And then it happened again.

"Another shell came aboard. Remember, we had never a chance to fire a single round out of those peashooters we were carrying. This one finished us. It blew the boiler and live steam shot over the decks, and it seemed that we were breaking in two in the middle. Someone gave the command to abandon ship, and we managed to get two boats manned and away. The Captain would not leave until they brought the Admiral and lowered him still in his wicker chair into one of the boats.

"It was now to row ashore and get to the shelter of the caves. We stopped to pick up some swimmers along the way, soon becoming overcrowded and having to let others hang on to us as we went on to the shore."

Silence again as everyone drank.

"And when we unloaded there in the cave, we found that the Admiral, miserable one, had died from his wound.

"We unloaded him there just as he was, wicker chair and all. In his chair, we left him sitting there in the sand, for about that time we discovered a band of *insurrectos* coming along the fields and not one of us had a weapon. You know what they would have done to us."

A brown hand drawn along his throat.

"So, we left him sitting there dead. Soon an American boat came along picking up our men who had taken shelter in the caves. They rescued us from the danger of the *Cubanos* and everybody forgot about the Admiral. Maybe they didn't forget about him but, after all, he was dead.

"Still, I myself cannot stop thinking about him sitting there in his chair. *Cosa fantastica—¿Verdad?*"

The next morning when General Wood came down to breakfast he found Lieutenant McCoy wrapped in contemplation of a map of the harbor, and when he inquired as to his interest in it, heard the Pilot's story of the battle.

He pondered. "Get our boat ready for Sunday morning, McCoy," he said. "We'll take a cruise around those caves and see if there is any truth in the fantastic tale you've picked up."

And so it happened.

They found Admiral Villamil exactly as the pilot of the torpedo boat had described him, still sitting as he had been left, dead in his chair. General Wood had the body of the gallant Admiral brought down to Havana, embalmed and placed in a coffin, and Lieutenant McCoy was sent to contact the former Spanish Governor and to ask him to take charge of it.

But the Governor refused, saying that he now had no connection with the Spanish government and lacked the authority to act. Any such proceeding would have to await the naming of a new envoy and his arrival in Cuba.

In the meantime, having no other place to store the coffin, it was sent to the Ordnance storehouse as being the nearest and most accessible, and it awaited the planned transfer.

Quite the most formidable of all the property returns submitted by our Army, in those days, the Ordnance return, which had to be submitted twice a year, was the absolute top. It was carefully audited both at Field Headquarters and in Washington and could well become the center of a full half-year's correspondence, if it were poorly made out. One regulation, in particular, had to be literally interpreted and obeyed.

This was to the effect that any property not listed on the return and not covered by invoice must be taken up under the heading, "Found at Post or Station." Officers were coming from and going to the States at a great rate; for that always is the situation at the end of a campaign and it was so here in Havana. Consequently, there were many changes in Ordnance officers, and each time the responsibility for the property in the Ordnance storehouse was changed, an inventory had to be made. The first one had resulted in the body of the unfortunate Admiral becoming Ordnance property, for he appeared on the Ordnance return as "Found at Post."

The item took the form of "1 (one) Admiral, Spanish," and then in parenthesis the word "dead" so that the whole thing read "1 (One) Admiral, Spanish (dead)."

And so it went, with too many things requiring action and the complete attention of those responsible, that no one took the trouble to change it.

And, in time, a new Spanish Consul did arrive from Madrid. He was a man of fine personality and became a favorite with the Americans in no time at all. It was inevitable that Lieutenant McCoy should tell the story at table one night, and years later he told me ruefully, "I'm afraid that I told it with a certain amount of undue levity for the newly arrived Consul became quite excited."

"Villamil?" his face lighted up.

"You have the body of Admiral Villamil?

"This is a thing most important. In Spain there has been no proof of his death. His family is entitled to many things from the Government, if it is proved that he died in action. Then there is his estate, which has never been settled. His family needs the help, too, for lacking a settlement of the estate they are finding it hard to live on what is available. It is my duty to the family, which I well know, as well as to my Government to get his body back to Spain."

And here General Wood stepped in. With his usual grace, he offered on behalf of the United States to return the body to Spain, saying that he was certain that the United States would confirm his offer. You will probably recall that this was done with a will for all the Spanish dead were returned.

So the body of Admiral Villamil, along with the others recovered, was escorted to the famous *Olympia* and taken back to Madrid where his erstwhile foes marched in the official funeral escort.

And the item on the Ordnance Return of the Havana Ordnance Depot "1 (One) Admiral, Spanish (dead)" appeared for the last time. I have always had a certain secret admiration for the resourceful Ordnance officer who closed out this item forever by writing under the column headed "remarks" the entry "Returned to Consignor."

Tropical Democracy

Although, I never had the pleasure of serving in the Caribbean, I spent eight years along the coast of West Africa and can relate to the climate, the primitive conditions, and the people of the kind mentioned in this story. Once again this is a story told me by my father who was stationed in Panama while the Canal was under construction. Those were wild times with U.S. Army, U.S. Navy; men from Barbados and other Islands; Indians, Panamanians; criminals; murderers; preachers; etc., all mixed together.

This particular story deals with the U.S. government's attempt to hold the first open election in Panama, and it is one of the most delightful stories of this collection of my father's stories.

Tropical Democracy: A Fair and Square Election

The Plaza Central was as empty as it ever gets, for the sun was now high and it was getting hot.

The trade winds still blew cool in the shade and the palm trees bowed gracefully to them.

Hibiscus blossoms nodded a vivid greeting and the tropical *softness* hung peacefully over us.

I was watching a man, who like me, was idling on a bench well back in the park's secluded corner, and so was partially hidden. He was well out of the way of the dust and the torn pieces of discarded lottery tickets, which came with the breezes and fluttered past the shrill-voiced children playing some game or other.

His eyes, set well apart in a thin face, were as blue as the Caribbean sky; his light tan suit, with matching buck shoes, was immaculate and the pointed small mustache, gray as it was, gave him a jaunty time-defying look. A new Panama rested firmly on a shock of gray hair.

When he moved at all, his motions were quick and alert.

Sight as he was, it was not his appearance alone, which held my interest; it was the little song he kept whistling to himself that did it. I remembered that song for many a time we had, as Lieutenants of Cavalry, roared it out. I had a crazy impulse to sing the words to his tune:

> And then she went to Kansas City
> Hi Ho the Rolling River...

and when he hit the chorus, I did sing aloud:

> We're bound away for the wild Missouri.

He turned and looked me over carefully; then a smile mounted clear to his eyes. "I should have known," he chuckled, "you were of the old *Prepare to Mount, Mount,* school. What are you doing now?"

"I work here, Colonel, on the Canal."

"Do you, now? There were many songs of this place too. Some a little lurid. The first builders used to sing:

> There was I a-working in the ditch;
> a-getting' the spiggoty itch; poor old...

He stopped singing abruptly; "We used to teach it to the Blacks from Martinique and Haiti. It had more snap when sung with an accent."

He turned and faced the corner. "There used to be a café over there, the *Café Central.* All of us from Las Cascadas used to frequent it, especially on dance nights at the Tivoli."

"It's still there, Colonel."

"Well, I move that we adjourn to it. It's getting a little hot and it's not too early, do you think?"

So that is how I started the day, by drinking beer, Balboa Best Beer Brewed, at eleven in the morning.

The café was empty and pleasantly cool. As we entered, the Colonel attracted general interest by speaking to each *niozo* in the kind of Spanish spoken in the Zone. He guessed accurately that the bartender was Curacoan and spoke pleasantly to him in his native *Papamiento,* that bizarre combination of Spanish, English, Portuguese, Dutch and Carib—the despair of all foreigners.

With the beer dewing the sides of our glasses, we reminisced.

He had come originally to the Zone with the first Army troops to be sent there. They had been hastily gathered together for the change of station and had come from San Antonio, Texas, way back in 1911. The mission given them was to defend Panama and the Canal, which was well on its way. I gathered that this quick change was a matter for self-defense on the Army's part for unless Army quickly put a force in being in Panama, the Navy, with its Army of Marines was ready to freeze the Army out.

"We were none too happy about this change of station," he went on, "for we were living under the most difficult conditions our troops had met since '98.

"We had expected to find a post, no matter how sketchy—either partly completed or under construction—a welcome thought to us who had been living under canvas for years along the border, but no such luck.

"A battalion of Marines, under Major Smedley Butler, had arrived earlier and had built themselves into a passable post; but such was not for us.

"Since no post had been contemplated at the time the Army Appropriations Act had been prepared, no money had been set up, and our engineers on the canal, as well as the members of the Isthmian Canal Commission, who lived in neatly rowed tropical quarters, were not concerned. They refused us all construction materials, even a pound of nails; so we were busy wrecking the old French laborers' quarters and re-erecting them into troop barracks, store rooms, and so on, but not repeat not, for officers' quarters.

"The old Army tradition held; we were to be the last taken care of. The War Department had a simple solution for the quarters problem—married officers were forbidden to bring their families."

"We used to wonder," I broke in, "what a peace time regiment would be like without any women in it. We bachelors were pretty well agreed that life for us would become easier, for all the married officers would have to do full duty instead of wishing work on the juniors while they took wifey shopping."

"Well, that's so, to a degree," he admitted, "but it is easy to understand the bachelor's position. Unlike me, you are young enough to belong to this era when marriage is part of the academic curriculum, so to speak, and most Second Lieutenants report for duty with a bride hooked onto their pistol belts. As to what a regiment was like without women, one of our Lieutenants established a local reputation as a wit by saying, after a particularly gruesome Cavalry exercise, that we would have a fine bunch, if it were not for the men and the horses. He didn't dare mention the women."

"There was a time when you found out about the lack of men and horses after World War I, wasn't there?" I couldn't help noodling him. "As I recall it, the Army was so reduced in strength that it was hard to find."

"Yes. That was an awful period. But we are straying, and to return I was saying that they were building quarters, making roads, fighting back the jungle, which is always on the point of recovering the little areas taken away from it, and is damnably persistent about it.

"At the same time trying to care for our administration and following the instructions issued from Washington and from Governor's Island, then the Headquarters of the Eastern Department under which we were working. I'm afraid we were making heavy weather of it.

"Right in the middle of the rainy season, with practically everything we had on endless fatigue, early one afternoon the Headquarters bugler sounded 'Officers' Call.'

"We dropped everything and were off to report. You can imagine the effect on every man of us. Even the guard house gang stood amazed. All of us hoped secretly that there was a war somewhere far away from the Zone with all its work, and that we had been selected as the first to go.

"At Headquarters, we milled around in the office of the Sergeant Major, waiting to be summoned into the Colonel's presence. Each one asked the new arrivals 'What the hell has happened?'

"No one knew.

"We finally sat, sweated, scratched, and waited to be sent into the inner office. The air soon became saturated with that hot, acrid, sour sweaty smell, which emanates from the white man in the tropics.

"Soon the Colonel, preceded by the Adjutant, emerged. We rose as one man and stood at attention. We gazed fixedly at the short, stocky figure of our CO who for all his fifty years, showed energetic activity.

"The center button on his blouse showed some strain and his usual calm was obviously the result of long practiced self-control. His naturally ruddy complexion was now well bleached by too much tropics and was somewhat more pasty than usual. His manner was sharply military.

" 'I have brought you here to give you personally a very unusual mission. I shall be as brief as I can. You all know that the natives here are not very firm politically. They are kept politically dumb by their exploiters, the village officials and the police who have traditionally gouged them. It is quite likely that unless those in the back country can be taught the power of their ballots to control and improve their lives, they will be taught eventually to extort from us and will become our enemies.

" 'It may well be that such an attitude, coupled with the penchant of the Anglo-Saxon for giving away his prerogatives, will force some sort of show down on our strategically important Canal. So, this mission I am giving you may well be of first import.

" 'Just a few hours ago, there was handed to me by the U.S. Minister here, in Panama, this telegram'—he waved it in the air like a guidon—'which states that the U.S. undertakes to guarantee to the Panamanians that the approaching election will be conducted on a fair and square basis and that this regiment will provide sufficient supervisory personnel to ensure it.'

"The CO's thick eyebrows rose and fell spasmodically and his face grew a bit ruddier.

" 'This is not a good time for us to handle such a job in our stride—rainy season, building barracks for the men, clearing the jungle and so reducing our fever rate. I don't relish losing you for some time, but there it is.

" 'It's not,' he went on, 'as though we are at war strength, or that this country is very friendly, or frankly hostile. You will be watchful and prepared for anything.

" 'To those of you who don't speak Spanish, our Ministry will provide an interpreter. Each officer will have considerable riding to do to cover all his polling places, so you will each take one orderly and one cook from your units.'

"He went on with some additional administrative instructions to the Adjutant to assign areas and furnish lists of polling places; the Quartermaster to provide transportation and so on. But at the end, with grave impressiveness, the CO said 'In many ways these people are primitives, but they are very sensitive. You must head them in the right direction for Democratic government.'

"Well," said the Colonel, "it worked about as we thought it"—he smiled wryly—"we went out in reverse order of rank, for once. The lowest powered went farthest. There were not enough officers and we used the senior Sergeants, keeping them at places nearest the Post so that said could be quickly forthcoming.

"As for me, I was next to low man on that totem pole and you can imagine where I went.

"When our orders came they were disgustingly specific. We (the lowest ranking five) were to sail on a Spanish coasting vessel, the *Estrella del Oeste*, up the Pacific side. This was a break for us, for travel by sea was much easier than fighting through the jungle over the coastal rivers in the rainy season.

"Lack of ports meant very little, for the shallow draft of the *Estrella* allowed her to stand in so close that we could swim and wade ashore if necessary.

"The exciting part of the order was the paragraph assigning areas and listing polling places, which we had to visit during the balloting and some little time before the election. A little study brought disillusionment. It didn't take much figuring with the aid of the schedules of all the coasting steamers schedules to discover that while there was a month between the primary and the final election, there was not enough time for those of us farthest out to get back to the Post and return to our areas before the finals. Once out, we stayed till the end.

"The next few days were full of activity for all of us. Rations and supplies to be drawn and made up for the pony transportation; instructions for the assistant cooks who may have never seen the inside of a kitchen before; selection of the other men for the detail—men who could be trusted alone in the jungle towns, hunters for the most part; and a general brushing on available maps; followed by a more or less complete orientation on election laws and customs, given by representatives of our Ministry.

"The Medical help we were to get was of somewhat sketchy character. The Regimental Medico—there was only one his assistant being long overdue—was to make trips out of Panama city to the various Headquarters towns, as water transportation became available; and we were to carry with us a package of drugs, salves, pills (both starters and stoppers), quinine, all properly labeled as to identification and dosage and we were to be our own help-yourself diagnosticians. There were bandages against cuts and broken bones, and last, but by no means least in this array of goodies, was one quart bottle (this was before the day of the fifth) of good old hospital whiskey. Hippocrates could not have asked for more.

"The Ordnance Officer was very businesslike. He issued us fifty rounds of ammunition per rifle, a hundred extra for hunting, gave us his blessing and his plans for replenishment; absolved us from having to return the empty cartridge cases and retired grumbling to his bunk in bachelor quarters, a transformed ward in the old French hospital.

"The Finance Officer bowled us over. He bestowed upon us one hundred dollars in acceptable U.S. money for which we signed and were told that we must return in balancing receipts for any amounts spent, and furthermore, there would be no release from accountability for these funds until such receipts were forthcoming.

"One Officer volunteered the information that in the area to which he was going there was only one man who could read or write and he was the village priest. The Finance Officer was pleased.

"'Let him sign for everybody,' he said. 'That's easy.'

"The night before we were to sail was depressing. The doctor sat in our midst giving us to understand that we were not to open our drug packages before we left. As usual, it had been raining; the palms and banana fronds leaked water onto the roof of our lean-to and it had run impartially down the galvanized iron sheets on either side so that for a few inches around the inside of the room, the floor was sopping wet.

"You know how hot it gets, right away after a shower in the rainy season, and how the humidity makes it torture to wear a raincoat. The skies were clearing and the brilliant stars of the tropic nights were hanging like lanterns against the gray black of the sky. The night sounds of the jungle were renewing and the cat animals were out again. The deep throated air-hammer sound the iguana makes was coming in loud and clear and it occurred to me that within the next few days, I might be on an iguana diet, broken by an occasional deer steak or a fish; clearly my diet could well be a function of my hunting and fishing skills.

"It was all to the good to get away from this bedraggled garrison where each day was a lot like yesterday and where in spite of constant hard work, we seemed no better off, nor more comfortable. I re-read my instructions for the twentieth time and hoped for the best.

"There was only one afternoon train from the wrong side of the Canal Post into Panama, and we looked forward to the five or six hours on our own in the city before we had to embark. Captain Hammer was in charge and inspected the baggage as it was piled at the station ready for loading. He had had much Philippine experience and was an idol of all the Lieutenants; a fine soldier, well versed in all things an officer was required to know. Of medium height and well set up, he had the clearest brown eyes I have ever seen and within their depths lurked a humor, which flashed out when least expected. His great charm of manner as well as his bachelor status made him much sought after when it came to having certain female visitors to the Canal.

"1 LT Rockey, Second In Command, like Captain Hanner, had done much jungle fighting in the Philippines. He had started as a Cadet at West Point and had been there a year or so, when mathematics, upon which much emphasis was placed, caught him up. He had come up through the ranks in the Cavalry to his commission. It was our unanimous belief that he was a brilliant and resourceful soldier. Physical condition was a fetish for him. His clear blue eyes and his know-how made him stand out in our regiment.

"LT Kurtz had brought along his hammock. He never slept on the ground where insects or snakes could get at him for he believed that any abrasion, scratch or bite, which penetrated the skin was an open invitation to all manner of loathsome genus. We used to kid him about it, but we knew that he was right.

"The rest of us were simple run-of-the-mine 2 LTs: Hatch, Bertsy, and myself. We had done much hunting there in the Zone and in the back country and were quite confident of our abilities to cope with it.

"The enlisted contingents handled the loading and were invited to ride in the baggage car. This was a real favor for they could relax opposite the open door in the cooling rush of the breezes.

"Our first care upon arriving at the Tivoli Hotel was to rent a room where we could strip off our saturated clothing and get cooled off. To make certain that such a condition would last, each opened his package of drugs and removed his quart of hospitality whiskey. Hatch spoke for all of us when he offered the thought that when and if we became sick in the jungle we might be so badly off we wouldn't appreciate what we were getting; or, worse still we might come down with something for which whiskey might be fatal, thus, no one would ever know what happened. Anyway, we decided to drink what we could of the whiskey before embarking and to save the rest for emergency drinking.

"A few of our friends, staying at the Tivoli, came up to see what the garrison news might be and we found that there had been published in the daily paper an interview with the Ministry which told of the generous offer of the U.S. to guarantee a 'fair and square' election and of what the regiment was doing to ensure it. Nothing had been omitted.

"We read it and enjoyed our brief glory.

"Someone suggested a poker game with the remaining whiskey as stake, bottle by bottle. Hatch ended up with all that were left.

"The arrival of additional guests broke up the game and the stakes were consumed. So went the afternoon and after a good supper, we became a bit uneasy about the enlisted contingents waiting for us at the wharf and we departed for the *Estrella*.

"We found the ship without difficulty—she was the only one at the wharf lighted with lanterns. On guard over the baggage piled amidships was a Corporal and two men. The rest of the contingent had gone for supper, but were expected back any minute.

"Captain Hanner summoned me to help him find the Skipper of the *Estrella* and to act as interpreter, if one was needed. One was.

"The Skipper looked thoughtfully out over the calm bay, spat in the water and said, 'We will sail at ten.' I translated. Captain Hanner said to me 'Wanna bet?' I said 'No.' The interview ended.

"Captain Hanner, on our way back to the wharf, allowed that he had known many like that Skipper and that there was no one in the engine room. He was not convinced that we would sail much before midnight, if then. In all this he was wrong.

"The Captain instructed the Lieutenant, and the enlisted contingent, that we were to sail at nine o'clock, and that was fine by my reckoning. I am not confirming any 'hurry up and wait' Army attitude, which you may have observed in your military service, but in these cases one had to anticipate the unexpected and needed elbow-room.

"It was about nine o'clock when the sound of singing burst upon us, and gradually swelled louder and louder. As it became clearer, I realized that there was a strong soprano section. All of us went to the rail and looked down on the loading area, fully lighted by the lanterns, now the objective of the marching chorus.

"They were singing a simple Spanish ditty of the country, with words a little on the peppery side. I feel certain that it would not have been heard in the drawing rooms of the aristocracy of Spain and Spanish America, but all the *paisanos* gathered as passengers knew it and joined heartily in the refrain.

"It was certain that the soldiers and interpreters had joined forces and the catalytic agent was none other than the Demon Rum, washed down with what looked and smelled like sweet Vermouth. The place simply reeked of it. It is not too bad a drink when well cooled, but it is practically murder, out of a bottle on a hot night at our temperature.

"The soprano section was quite polyglot and was a from a cross section of Cocoa Grove, the center of the area marked on the city map hanging in the Provost Marshal's office 'off limits for soldiers.'

"There were French gals, native Panamanians, (a few from the Bayano River Country); Costa Rica was represented, as were Honduras, Trinidad, Martinique and Haiti; figures and colors *al gusto*, and all inclined to relapse into their own languages in the intervals between songs.

"Some, seeking greater comfort, had taken off their shoes and were carrying them slung around their necks. Tastes in dress were as varied as the women, but generally there was a cheerful colored waist and, gathered snugly around the hip; a skirt of some dark material, which against the sea's background, or fluttering from the shadows, produced an effect like that of a flock of parroqueets.

"Under the baleful glare of the Sergeants our enlisted contingent gradually withdrew from the party and began to appear singly or in pairs on the deck. The baggage disappeared into the hold, and none of us could think of leaving this colorful gathering to itself. The interpreter, and a few of the legitimate passengers, brought a half 'paulin out from one of the sheds; a guitar appeared from nowhere and obviously there was to be a *baile*.

"The Skipper gravely descended from the pilothouse and greeted the women on the wharf enthusiastically, calling many by name. One tall brunette passed him a bottle and he drank deep with his head tilted back so far that his hat seemed suspended from its *embocadero*. He finished with a loud 'hoof' of appreciation. I expected to see him take off in some sort of a fiery cloud, but he stood steadying himself against a bollard, while he meditated.

"'If our friend, the Skipper, can get away with that drink combination, he has the steadiest head in Panama,' muttered Captain Hanner, at my elbow. He went on to elaborate on our chances of getting away at any time before morning.

"'The guy is hell bent on borrowing trouble it seems. Here we have all the elements, which spell trouble with a big 'T'—rum, women, and a hell of a lot of temperament. Well, it will serve him right; but we are definitely not a part of this picture.

"'Did you, by chance, ever run the engines of such an antique vessel as this?'

"I hadn't.

"Captain Hanner swore disgustedly into the darkness and we resumed our places at the rail, for the show below.

"The guitarist ran a scale and struck a few chords. We saw our Skipper let go the bollard, reach for the brunette and gallantly return her bottle. He laced both hands on her hips and they began to dance on the 'paulin.

"At first, we held the Skipper's dance in some derision; for his bent knees, up thrust chin and yellow shirt, with its frayed collar, gave him all the grace of a lively scarecrow, but as the rum took hold, he grew more confident and relaxed, and danced much better.

"But his inspiration was his partner. She followed closely and gracefully, dancing with her whole body—her feet followed the music, and her hands, held high above her damp hair, swayed with the dance. Those powerful brown arms, sloping into broad hands with long tapering fingers, emphasized the sinuosity of her body and her whole dance held invitation.

"A third figure sprang out of the shadows and onto the 'paulin. He was greeted by the applause of the whole company and his name went the rounds. It was Luis something or other. Our soldiers, too, seemed to know him and applauded. He brushed the Skipper aside and took up the dance without skipping a measure.

"His partner smiled seductively and there began the best performance I've ever seen. It was real grace; the music changed tempo and the dancers changed with it. The thump of bare feet on the canvas was in perfect rhythm and the bare feet of the audience took it up.

"The man, Luis, snatched at his shirt and tossed it free to one of the women in the crowd. His partner followed suit and her blouse joined his. The audience roared its appreciation and the two dancers, nude to the waist, continued. The music came louder and faster and the audience shifted nervously and cheered.

"Captain Hanner looked over his Lieutenants. 'Unless you can take this in your stride,' he said, 'you're not fit to hold down a job like the one you're going on, where you have to live in a small jungle town.'

"I marked that his eyes kept moving to the shadows in the outer circle of the group. He asked me to point out the Skipper, who had now gone back to leaning on his bollard. The look with which the Skipper was watching Luis was unmistakable and we saw him call a man from the crowd and send him along the wharf. Captain Hanner nudged me.

"'The damned traitor! He's up to some devilment. We may get off sooner than I thought. He's selling this lot down the river.'

"Suddenly one of the women screamed loudly and the dance stopped. '¡Policia! ¡Policia!' she yelled, and ran for the nearest exit to the street.

"The Skipper, from below, yelled at the top of his lungs for all passengers and interpreters to get aboard. That half of the crowd nearest the ship, made for the gangway, and the dancers, swept up in the mass, went with them. We could all hear them settling down on the lower deck like a flock of shore birds on a sand bar.

"The Skipper yelled to the police that the ship was now sailing, that all the passengers were *bona fide* ones and that he was carrying a large body of *soldados Americanos* north to supervise the elections.

"He then took his place in the pilothouse, and jangled to the engine room. The police helped the last crew member loosen the lines and get them aboard and we slowly slid out into the bay.

"Captain Hanner looked at his watch. It was exactly ten thirty. 'Not bad,' he grinned, 'Not at all bad. But things are not so good for that Skipper. Both those dancers are aboard and unless he can think up some way to get rid of them peacefully, fairly close to Panama City, they'll make him wish he'd never been born—especially when there is no more rum. At that, they are better off than the others. The police probably had the exits all covered and will levy a fine of twenty *pesos* or so for creating a disturbance and that money goes straight into their pockets.'

"Kurtz slung his hammock between the corner of the pilothouse and the stumpy mast and turned in. The rest of us, having searched out a cleared space large enough for it, followed suit.

"It was close to midnight when Captain Hanner awakened me in the fashion we had been taught to do in the jungle, that is by grasping the wrist loosely and hanging on. As soon as he knew I was awake, he growled, 'Come along and help me wake the others.'

"The little *Estrella* was really rolling in the roughening sea. The moon had disappeared behind a thick mass of clouds and the long oily roller seemed to flow backwards as the ship settled into the troughs to rise again in a sickening roll and shake herself over the crests.

"Only Kurtz was still asleep. The rest were gathered in the lee of the pilothouse, hanging onto a line stretched along the side. Kurtz's hammock swung across the little deck from one side to the other, and for part of its swing was out over the water. When we had managed to awake him, his surprised look of terror amused no one, but he managed to drop to the deck and roll into the scuppers on one of those awful lurches of the ship at the top of her roll.

"The rain began—a fine chilling rain, quite common in tropical storms where it rains not quietly and decently but over-enthusiastically. The pilothouse offered but little shelter and we were thoroughly chilled. Our running lights were burning bright and in the light of the steerman's lantern we could see two figures inside the pilothouse, one in the dingy yellow blouse of the Skipper.

"Captain Hanner stood in the center of the group in the lee of the pilothouse. 'A rough night. I'd feel a little better about it if I had more confidence in that be-damned Skipper up there. I'm no sailor at all, but I'll risk a small bet that he has no more idea of where he is than I have.

This is a flat, sandy shore along here and it's easy enough to go ashore opposite the mouth of one of these rivers. There is a long bar in front of everyone. You come along with me and I'll ask him.'

"We went up a little gangway leading to the pilothouse and found the Skipper, who showed great interest in the group of officers who came along with us. Captain Hanner asked the question and I translated.

"'Do you know where we are now?'

"'Certainly.'

"'Well, where are we?'

"He put his finger on a greasy little chart of the Pacific Coast of Panama—it wasn't much larger than the palm of my hand, and in the dim light of the lantern was perfectly illegible—'Right there,' he said vehemently. His finger must have covered some fifty nautical miles of coastline.

"Captain Hanner snorted. 'Ask the bastard how he knows.'

"The Skipper nodded in satisfaction. He took an unlighted lantern from its bracket and descended to the deck. We all followed him along the deck and down a companionway to his little cabin. Everyone crowded in and the Skipper struck a match to light the lantern. It promptly blew out. We then gathered round to form a windbreak with our raincoats and finally he managed to light it. We were so packed in that we were hardly disturbed by the ship's roll. The Skipper paused for effect.

"'What's he going to do?' asked Rockey, who up to that time had been silent. Captain Hanner shrugged 'Ask him,' he nodded to me. The Skipper was the center of attention and enjoying it.

"'I will now,' said he, 'show your officer that I am fully aware of our location and will be glad to explain to him. This ship is equipped in the most modern fashion and its officers are well instructed,' I translated.

"'Oh, Christ,' said Captain Hanner.

"With that, the Skipper got down on his knees, searching for something and I must confess that I knelt beside him. He groped beneath the little bunk, turning his head to one side, and brought forth a brass bound mahogany box. He motioned the group of us back, for he needed more room, and then opened wide the box and swung his lantern well over it.

"I don't know what I expected to see, but certainly not what we did see. A full sized mariner's compass filled the box; and the card was swinging merrily in complete circles around in it.

"We gazed, spellbound and then looked from one to another. The Skipper without hesitating proudly closed the box and replaced it under the bunk.

"I looked at Captain Hanner, expecting some sort of an outburst to end all outbursts, but gravely he circled the group with a blank face, until his eyes met Rockey's grin. They both burst out roaring with glee and, as the Skipper retired in all dignity, their bursts of laughter filled the cabin and reached the deck.

"'Oh, hell,' from Captain Hanner, 'that was a sight. All of you hanging over that damned compass with your mouths wide open. That will surely be the last act in this night's show. It's bad enough to be at sea on a night like this, but with that crazy Skipper it's a lot worse. Up on deck now, before he comes back to give us another lesson in seamanship.'

"'In the morning,' the Colonel continued, 'the weather cleared and broad daylight found us standing in to Anton, the first port, where we were to drop Captain Hanner. We helped him get ready to debark and were sorry to see him go. A dory sized boat stood off our bow waiting and the oarsmen were talking animatedly to the Skipper. It was clear that some sort of a deal had been made. The exact kind was evident when the dancer and her partner of last night appeared to go ashore too. The girl dropped lightly into the boat followed by Luis; a volley of *Adios* crackled alongside and both helped Captain Hanner to his place in the stern.

"I leaned over the *Estrella's* side and quoted as exactly as I could, the impressive speech of our Commanding Officer back there in Las Cascadas.

"'In many ways these people are primitives, but they are very sensitive. You must head them in the right direction for democratic government, Captain, Sir.'

"Captain Hanner leered up at me. 'To a people whose course is set by what they keep under a bunk, any direction is the right one. And as for you, little man, remember to keep your little rifle where you can reach it and out of the way of the itchy fingers of these very sensitive people.'

"He disappeared towards the shore and the little jungle town where he was to be law, equity and order for the elections."

The Colonel sighed, called for the bill; and to my question about the outcome of the election said that they had gone off very well. It was true that in one or two of the districts it had become necessary to lock the police in their own jails for a time, but they had been released when the voting was finished.

His train was due to depart for Colon and he took a waiting taxi.

It was not until after he had gone that I realized that I didn't know his name.

The Championship

The fighter, to which this narrative refers, is Harry Webb—pound for pound one of the great fighters in boxing history. He fought in a wide range of weights from 147 to 165. At one time, he was the Welterweight Champion of the World and later the Middleweight Champion also. Later on in the early 20's he fought Gene Tunney—who later defeated Jack Dempsey twice to become the Heavyweight Champion to a close loss.

I'm not sure that my father, who wrote this narrative, knew that Henry Webb who was the hero of the story was really Harry Webb picking up what he thought were going to be some easy dollars.

It's a great story!

The Championship

We had all been to see the prizefights.

The fleet had sent out its champions and the local army garrisons had met them fairly. The fights had been thoroughly enjoyed by all the veteran soldiers and sailors not on guard or on some other inopportune duty for which a terrorized recruit could not be substituted.

There we sat on the upstairs porch of the Howard Hotel with a bottle reminiscent of older days. A soft summer breeze blew up from the Bay and we relaxed into real comfort.

The Major reached for his glass and sighed, "I don't know," he began, "why I ever go to see fights any more. It must be a habit. I think I've already seen the most interesting sporting events in the world—two in number, and one of them was a prize fight."

"Go on, Major," we all chorused. "Let's have it," for the Major when surrounded by a company of those who are honored by being classed as his friends, delights in telling a story and we with him have never been disappointed in its telling.

The Major laughed softly, sat back in his chair and with the mellow lights of the city merrily winking at us we heard the story.

"It was some years ago, perhaps more than most of you can remember, that I was stationed in Panama. I went with the first troops to go for station and what with the Engineers, Marines and other specimens of voracious insect life, living was inclined to be hectic for the poor but honest soldier man.

"We had no houses or barracks at first. Washington was slow in answering our calls for fluids and for construction materials. We simply dawdled along.

"Our morale was considerably lowered. The regiment to which I then belonged was one of our best—at least we all considered it so and since no military instruction or training was possible without clearing a space for it in the tangled jungle, as invariably happens, discipline became lax and what with a minimum of drill and a maximum of hard labor, we had our troubles.

"The Colonel of the regiment was a tried and experienced campaigner. He knew instinctively that we were in for it and while he was fighting Washington on the one hand to get construction materials for us, on the other hand he fought the terrible homesickness which tropical semi-isolation brings to men. His greatest endeavors to this end were centered in a drive for athletics and not having a baseball field, naturally most of our efforts became centered on boxing.

"Boxing is a good time for everybody, if you exclude the poor devil who is on the losing end. To our great surprise, we found that our native friends, the Panamanians liked it. They were present at all the battalion and regimental bouts. Being then a 2LT, and the latest from the Point, it was no more than natural that I should be put in charge of athletics and I certainly took my job seriously.

"Our Panamanian friends soon began to desert their cock fights and come in to see *Los combates*, particularly when they found that a little gambling on a favorite would not be frowned upon and that gambling was a vocation in which our soldiery showed great skill and sportsmanship.

"All this, you must understand, was occurring at the same time the Canal was being constructed. There were some pretty hard kiddies on the construction crews. Our fighters, as they developed, began to cast around looking for easy money and of course that gave me considerable entrée into the local boxing circles. I would always furnish a fair fighter on short notice, and since the Army was regarded as the acme of all things fair and square, I was of considerable local reputation as an arbiter.

"One evening as the guest of a local club in company with three or four other officers from the regiment, I went to a fight. It was slow and the night was hot. I saw nothing to get enthusiastic about. Not so, one of the friends with me. He kept squirming about in his seat, and finally quite excited out of his ordinary self, pulled me over to him and half whispered, 'That blond youngster in the far corner is Henry Webb.'"

I sat up straight. Henry Webb was at that time one of the finest fighters who ever came from Pittsburgh. He was a contender for the Middleweight Championship of the World and he eventually won it.

The Major drank deeply from his glass and continued.

"At the end of our local fight which Henry won in an easy three rounds, my friend Hatch, killed at Cantigny, poor chap, introduced me to Henry Webb and for a kick of something else to do and to share our prize with our messmates, we brought Henry back to the Officers' Club with us. He turned out to be a really decent chap. He was traveling without a manager; had just come down to see the Canal between bouts, as it were, and decided to spend a few months there.

"He saw no reason why he shouldn't go ahead to make expenses while he was there and continue light training without having to pay for sparring partners. He was proceeding to box all corners in and out of his weight.

"He made us all promise to preserve his incognito. He was fighting under the name Kid Kilpatrick. We were very glad to enter his conspiracy and went to all his fights. I remember in Colón he once fought three gigantic Negroes in one afternoon. You know the kind. Muscles like steel cables standing out against the black skin and rippling with each movement.

"The recognized champion of the Isthmus at that time was a Mexican. Rodriguez, he called himself. A dirtier fighter I never saw. Whenever he felt that there was a good chance of his losing, he would deliberately foul. He would butt his opponent if possible and whenever he could, his favorite stunt was to crush the toes by stamping on them. He was a bull of a man with black tousled hair and unshaven jowls, and the one thing all the Americans in Panama enthusiastically looked forward to was a crushing defeat for *Señor* Rodriguez.

"Well, Kid Kilpatrick fought his way, slowly but surely, through many set-ups and contenders to the point where he could logically challenge the Champion of the Isthmus. Our regiment hugged itself in unholy glee.

"You know how things are in a regiment of Infantry. A few officers know something. The Regimental Sergeant Major finds it out—he swears the First Sergeants to secrecy and tells them; the First Sergeants swear the Sergeants to secrecy and tell them; and the next thing the entire regiment knows it and sits figuratively in on it.

"That was the way in this case. Kid Kilpatrick seemed confident, as well he might, but he advised caution.

"'You can never tell,' said he, 'what will happen in a prize fight. I can lick this Mexican all right: but there is no telling what the official verdict may be, you know referees. I'm hoping to clean up a little money and I'm putting up what little I have left over on myself, but I never advise any of my friends to bet on one of my fights.'

"We reassured him and got him to set the date for the fight so that it would be right after payday. This I arranged and I felt very fine about it. It was for the benefit of the enlisted men

"The day of the fight everything about our Post was deserted. Even the prisoners in the guardhouse were doing everything possible to get things get over quickly. The guard was practically solid with recruits.

"I saw the Regimental Sergeant Major on the crowded train for town and I suspected that he had practically the entire regimental pay roll for one month. He confirmed this suspicion and asked my opinion. I was very much flattered.

"A remarkable old man, he was, with snow-white hair and a thin esthetic face, which would have graced a saint. But he maintained the dignity of his rank in such a way that even in a hard-bitten regiment no soldier cared to cross him unnecessarily. He watched over and took care of us Second Lieutenants.

"We arrived in town hours before the fight. As usual it was hot and the afternoon soon made our clothes cling to us. We met many other officers at the University Club. We had much conversation, mostly concerning Henry Webb, and consumed many cocktails. Finally the bar boy got us to enter a horse drawn carriage and we were off to the fight.

"There's a smell about Panama City, which haunts me. Burning firewood, anisette, rum and many unclean smells. I remember that some one commented on it on the way. Fortunately for us delicate ones, the fight was held out of doors. The place was crowded and a clamoring in Spanish, English and Chinese greeted us as we jammed ourselves through to our reserved seats.

"Hot and perspiring we sat through three preliminaries. The crowd displayed uncanny interest in them though they didn't amount to much as fights.

"And finally came the main bout. The referee made the conventional announcements. Our man, quite unattended, entered the ring. He was greeted boisterously by all U.S. soldiers and sailors while the officers present applauded by clapping their hands.

"When the Mexican appeared, all hell broke loose. The Spanish and Chinese contingents were regarding this as a national affair. It was North America versus Central America.

"The gray-haired and venerable Sergeant Major leaned over to tell me, shouting at the top of his lungs, that he had successfully placed the money even. My hundred dollars was in it. He seemed to feel that his part in the fight was over and, fanning himself with his straw hat, he prepared to enjoy it.

"Our lad in his corner looked ready for business. Assisted by a heavy boy, palpitatingly red from heat and excitement, he was busy crowding his taped hands into a pair of boxing gloves. A crooked nosed second had appeared from nowhere. Squatted on a folding canvas seat he was keeping up a running conversation. The boxing gloves on, our blonde youth arose, shuffled his feet in some rosin dust in the corner, flexed his legs a few times by squatting on his heels and resumed his seat.

In the Mexican corner things were different. There were so many brown brothers gathered there that at first it was difficult to see the champion. Buckets, water bottles, small bottles with a pharmacist's mark on them were resting on the edge of the ring. Chattering like a bunch of parroquets at evening, this crew unlaced their man's shoes, laced them up again; loosened his belt, tightened it again; fanned him with a towel, sponged his back, dried him off carefully—and then repeated the dose.

"Finally the referee having caused him to remove certain excess tapes from his hands, they jammed them into his boxing gloves. The referee made his announcements again and the gong sounded.

"Our man started, in a flat footed lazy way, across the ring with outstretched hand ostensibly to shake hands. He was met by a nifty left jab which had it landed would have set him well back on his heels. It never got home.

"Then action started. At first it seemed slow. Our boy kept well away. No infighting yet where the Mexican's greater weight could help him. Feeling with a left jab. A try with a right cross. One-two to the face and stomach. The smack of gloves came clear of the cheers of the crowd.

"In the latter part of the first round, our boy seemed to change his attack. Satisfied no longer with a passive resistance, he started. One-two. The Mexican's head snapped back before a jab. One-two again. A clinch. The referee parted them and our boy dropped his arms. One-two. Again the

Mexican's head snapped back and the gong sounded.

"The excitement was still all in the Mexican's corner. Much chatter and sampling of bottles. Much fanning. The Champion turned loose a volley of excellent Spanish curses at his seconds. I noticed how red the left side of his body was becoming and I realized that our blonde boy was doing a lot of business.

"Well, the second round was like the first. All through our boy straightened him up and snapped his head back with jabs. His right kept working on the body. Clinches became more frequent. Our boy got an elbow in the eye and apparently was irritated by it. He complained to the referee at an obvious attempt with a knee. The referee warned the Mexican. The Mexican didn't look so good to me then. Our regiment was voiceless now and could emit only throaty yells of glee. The Spanish cheering had noticeably lessened.

"Then, taking advantage of my acquaintance with Henry Webb, I had arranged a private signal of my own. When Henry had arrived at the point in his fight where he could make a close estimate on the Mexican's ability to last, he was to let me know. At this point, I noticed the heavy boy in Henry's corner looking at me. When he saw he had my attention he raised four fingers. I, in turn, beckoned the venerable Sergeant Major who hastily left with an additional hundred of my money, with an equal amount of his own.

"The idea was to get big odds for it by betting that the Mexican would be knocked out in the fourth round.

"The third round was savage. They met in the center of the ring, toe to toe. Distance fighting. Infighting, fighting out of clinches; our boy faced it all the way. His grin had left him. He shot his left through the Mexican's guard carrying it with him. His right met the Mexican with a smack against his wet body that sounded like a pistol shot.

"Again, again, again he sat him back on his heels with straight lefts. It was getting harder for the Mexican to save himself by clinching. He couldn't pin Henry's arms. Henry was going like a machine. His freckled shoulders twisting, his lithe waist bending. No apparent effort, power and still more power.

"The soldiers and sailors recovered some voice and raised a delirious howl. The end was apparent and their anticipation was pleasant.

"The gong sounded. The referee slapped them both on the shoulders. They were in a clinch. Henry dropped his arms to his sides and turned his back. The Mexican relaxed of his support pitched forward. I opened my mouth to yell a warning. No good. As the Mexican recovered his balance he leaned to the right and with all his might smote Henry just below the right ear. Henry pitched forward, then went down on the canvas and lay still. My word! What a foul that was!

"The shock was too much for the referee. The expression on his face, which normally would have done credit to a bulldog, was one of absolute disbelief. Before he could say a word, however, Henry rolled over and sat up.

"I had a confused impression of Henry's tearing at the knots on his gloves with his teeth and pulling one knee up under him. Then he was up. He shook his gloves from him and they rolled clear across the ring. His eye was half closed where he'd been fouled by the elbow and the blood was slowly running down his face from skinned places made by his impact on the canvas.

"Then Henry sighted his prey. There's no other word for it, Gentlemen. He sighted his prey. His lips parted in a snarl and with his taped hands up he slithered across that ring without a sound. The referee saw his intention and grabbed him by an arm. He tried to reason with Henry and I heard him say something that sounded like, 'You won, Kid, don't...'

"Henry didn't take time to spread his feet. His left simply lifted the referee from the canvas and made him change ends. The referee slid to a prone position and lay still. The crowd was shocked to silence, but I heard the aesthetic Sergeant Major behind me say 'God, ain't that grand!'

"The Mexican yelled at his seconds. Three of them threw themselves valiantly in front. Smack. Henry's taped hands were like the hammer of Thor. Smack. Smack. Three seconds hit the floor so hard, it echoed. It was glorious.

"A few spectators leaped in from Henry's corner, but by now Henry had the Mexican. He also had shed his gloves, but it was all over in a second and he had joined his unconscious *compañeros* on the floor.

"For some unknown reason, and with a flash of inspiration, the time-keeper struck the gong. Henry gave one look towards his corner. The heavy boy, positively goggle eyed now, was driving back with hot words the few spectators who had entered. He beckoned to Henry and Henry walked over and swung on the ropes.

"His remarks would have done credit to a Pershing. Rocking forward on his toes with the light of battle still in his eyes, 'Anybody want any more?' hoarsely demanded Henry. 'Any more?'

"Well, I shook the clutch of the venerable Sergeant Major and surrounded by my shock troopers, the squad of regimental boxers, we rescued Henry and took him away. It was glorious fighting," the Major chuckled. "Fighting became general shortly afterward and I was glad to get away." He stopped, finished his glass and reached for his hat.

"Wait," I said, "What about your bets and what about the regiment? What was the decision?"

"Well," replied the Major, "that also is peculiar. There was no referee to make the decision so none was ever made. We tried to collect, but it would have taken a war to do it so we finally gave it up. The Sergeant Major was heartbroken. He used to send a post card every Christmas to Henry Webb."

Vive Le France

On this particular November night three British subalterns sat snuggled around a regulation issue, pot bellied, sheet iron stove which formed their only source of heat in the Officers' Room of the Officers' rest camp in Le Havre.

Two of them were on their way to England for a seven-day leave; the third was returning and naturally the talk centered about home and London and its attractions. The wind howled dismally outside, and dashed a cold driving rain against the side of the shack with such violence that through its shrunken sides small streams flowed down to the floor causing each officer in turn to raise his feet from the floor and place them on an adjoining chair.

There was a lull in the conversation during which each officer puffed thoughtfully upon his pipe. McBride, the youngest in appearance of the three, who was returning to the front, finally burst forth. "I saw Douglas in Leicester Square talking with some ladies. He seemed in fine form, quite recovered from his wound, and looking very fine indeed. He was with Lady K— and they presented a striking appearance. He is almost an object of worship among the people of London and his latest exploits seemed to have quite taken the people by storm, you know."

Kingsley, a black haired taciturn Artillery Officer whose thin studious face gave one the impression that he was living in a world apart, added thoughtfully, "He well deserves all the praise England can give him, and I believe that we will have to yield the palm to him. His last exploit struck me as being a really superhuman one, perhaps not so much in its accomplishment as in its conception.

"Because... in the accomplishment of a deed of that kind there is really such an extreme element of luck that when one emerges alive he really deserves very little credit; but the imagination and the quick grasp of a complex situation, which together form the basis for conception, is something entitling him to England's gratitude. I believe on the whole that it was one of the noblest deeds of the war."

Silence again fell upon the group. The third officer whose insignia showed him to be a LT of Aviation, spoke for the first time.

"Of course, you are right, Kingsley, the deed was one requiring remarkable nerve and all honor to the man who did it, but since we are talking shop I believe that the bravest deed of the war will not go to your friend, nor even, perhaps to our nation, because my firm belief is that I have seen the bravest deed of the war executed by a Frenchman."

The two other officers regarded him with calm deliberation, the younger finally grunted. "Not really? Tell it, do."

The aviator squirmed uneasily, cleared his throat noisily and, spreading his hands towards the sheet iron stove, began.

"This happened in 1915 upon the —— Sector. That was when I joined aviation and you will both remember what a devil of a year it was. It seemed that everything was against us. Our biggest pushes ended in a sea of mud; the Bosch counter-attacked in wonderful weather. We could not admit it, but we were giving way, our lines were a mine of spies and our intelligence department seemed to give us nothing but false reports for so long a time that they hesitated to give us any.

"The German Organization seemed impregnable, its espionage was certainly beyond reproach and it was winning for them. Our best agents were of no avail, and I being in rather good form, and knowing every inch of the Bosch lines, was chosen for this mission.

"In some sort of a way this work became more and more distasteful to me, I could not take my mind from the thought of these brave chaps going over and landing with no sort of a sporting chance. My good work in combat flying began to fall off so much so that I was given a respite from this work and a seven day leave to England. This, I would say, was not associated with my mission in landing spies behind the German lines, but was rather in the nature of a reward for the work I had done in combat, and everyone concerned took particular pains to impress me with this fact, until I reached a point where I began to believe that I was among the leading aces, and that my life was of a great deal of importance to our great country.

"Upon my return from leave, I was surprised to find myself detailed for another mission of spy planting. I was to leave the airdrome at 2:30 A.M. to fly about sixty kilometers, and land the spy behind the town of P——. As you may recollect, the country is very open, and an airplane can get down in fairly good shape.

"After dinner of the evening before, the Squadron Commander called me in and told me that under no circumstances was I to land my plane;

that my passenger would be provided with a parachute; and that I should cut my motor off gliding as far as possible. When over my proper objective, I should signal the passenger by raising my hand and then he should make the leap.

"When I awakened at 1:30 A.M. for coffee and instruction by the Squadron Commander prior to my flight, I was introduced to my spy passenger. While my motor was being tuned up, and preparations were being made, I looked him over rather carefully. As you may well imagine, I did not want a suspicious looking chap behind me some twenty-five kilometers behind the Bosch line.

"He turned out to be a Frenchman of some seventy odd years of age, and to my astonished gaze seemed a typical French peasant. His French was a patois that I failed to recognize, but to my questions he replied as closely as I could gather to following effect.

"Yes he was going to fly with *M'seau*. No, he had never been in an airplane before. Yes, he had seen one once in the air, but it was a German plane and had dropped bombs on his native village.

"Yes, it had indeed been a terrible thing and had killed many defenseless people. Yes, he had a parachute; no, he had never jumped, neither from an airplane, nor from a balloon, but—I can see his smile now—he had been carefully instructed as to its use by an expert, a brave man who had made many jumps.

"No, he had no arms, it was better so, why should a peasant carry arms? Equipment, yes, he had some—a sack containing bread and cheese, and a couple of wonderful peaches given him by the same French officer who had told him what was wanted.

"His talk then drifted to peaches, and the preparations having been completed, and our coffee finished, we got into my plane and started for the lines. I personally saw that the old man was as comfortable as it was possible to make him; that his parachute was properly harnessed; and with a roar from the good Rolls-Royce motor we started for the line.

"My mind was far from being on my work. I took my bearings automatically. The thought of that great-hearted peasant, and what he meant to do, sent chill after chill up my spine. I recollected my own first flight, made in bright daylight; it had been anything but pleasant. I recollected an attempt I had made to jump from a plane with a parachute, and I tried to picture the old man's terror and desperation.

"Now that I was in the air I could not dare to turn and look at him for I felt that if I should see him in such pitiable state of funk that I felt he must be in, I would funk myself. I am Irish, you see, and a bit temperamental.

"We finally arrived at the site where I planned to cut my motor and glide. We had successfully passed the line and not a sign of anti-aircraft had fired a shot. At the end of my glide, while I was about two thousand feet up, I tuned around and looked at the old man. He was as cold as ice; his face was as calm and benign looking as my own grandfather's.

I raised my hand, he straightened his parachute, took a couple of carrier pigeons under his arm, stood for an instant, straight upright and in the dim light I could see his lips forming the words *Vive La France*. A quick salute, and he jumped.

"That, my friends, is the bravest deed I have seen in this war."

The blond youngster coughed noisily, drew his pipe from his mouth, puffed a cloud of smoke towards the ceiling and drawled, "I say, did his blooming parachute open?"

The other shrugged his shoulders, "Don't know," he sighed, and silence again fell on this little group of men who risked their all.

Pecans

Captain James Bayle, who commanded I Company, Tenth U.S. Infantry, was a striking figure. A good six feet two inches in his stocking feet, his face seamed from exposure to the sands of the Texas border and the suns of the tropics, he had a disposition which would curdle milk.

Physically, he was one of the strongest men in the regiment and everybody knew it. Still, he was no swashbuckler, but kept much to himself—a bit withdrawn. His blue eyes could flash fire when he was aroused, and most men withdrew instinctively well out of range.

In the eyes of the Lieutenants he had one completely redeeming virtue; he was not difficult to serve with. He was generous with leaves and had even been known to take over the weekend duties of his Lieutenants when they very much wanted to get away. He was a bachelor, thus did not push off his duties pleading family necessities.

But his great vice was that there was nothing he enjoyed more than annoying his superiors. True, he usually did this after much consideration. His particular aversion was to the Inspector General who in those days made both an "Administrative" and a "Tactical" Inspection once or twice a year.

It was Captain Jim's belief that the Inspector General was a bootlicker, ignorant of having to do with the real business of soldiering; entirely out of place in the realm of tactics, but an expert in the Army Regulations.

These, Captain Jim averred, were especially reserved for damned fools and Second Lieutenants.

At the time, the regiment was stationed at Fort Benjamin Harrison. It was an excellent post; the Indianapolis people were hospitable, and the gals were pretty and generous.

It looked like a good year for the Tenth and indeed it was until the Inspector General came along to make the regular annual inspection.

I Company had done well enough in all the tests prescribed, the inspection was about finished, and the Lieutenants had begun to breathe audibly again. Still, there were omens—not all propitious. Captain Jim had tangled with the Inspector in the matter of preparation of Muster Rolls and their checking and the Inspector General had pulled the Army Regulations on him—his ultimate weapon—but, *mirabile dictu*, Captain Jim had won the bout.

The consensus of opinions, in the Lieutenants' Mess that night was that there were certain games which could well be lost by winning and that we had not finished with the matter.

The last of the inspections was scheduled for the following morning. It was to be an inspection of barracks and quarters with the men standing at their bunks.

Things were going well enough when the Inspector General, having been met by Captain Jim in his most military fashion, stopped to look at the rear of I Company's barracks.

Along the wall in the near distance was a row of pecan trees and the Inspector General, sighting along the row, turned to Captain Bayles.

"Do you have your men pick those pecans when they are ripe? I suppose, of course, you do."

"No, Sir. We certainly do not."

"You don't? Why not? The messes ought to appreciate them."

A note of belligerency crept into Captain Jim's voice.

"Not our job, Sir. We're soldiers."

Here the Inspector General simply blew his top. "Well, you will pick them," he roared, "I'll be back here to see that you have. D'you understand. I'll be back here in the fall."

Captain Jim admitted cheerfully that he understood and the inspection was resumed, but the atmosphere was a bit strained.

The Battalion Commanders, as well as the Regimental, were present, but took no part in the incident, but everyone gathered the impression that their ideas were not much different from Captain Jim's.

So, the Regiment went its way to the summer maneuvers: to target practice; to marching attacks and defense systems; to firing exercises; to all those forms of outdoor sport which is the Infantryman's lot.

After the return to barracks, with the inevitable letdown in training, and when the pecans were ripe, Captain Jim excused his Company from routine drills and carefully supervised the picking and sacking of the nuts. He informed the other Captains that he was putting them away for the winter and that their messes could count on I Company's store.

He had hardly completed the job when in came a wire from Washington conveying the depressing news that the Inspector General was on the way and that another inspection would be held the following day.

During the summer, Captain Jim had grown a luxurious beard of which he was very proud. It was a two-toned job of nut brown and gray and had the effect of extending his jutting chin so that he appeared more belligerent than ever. The Lieutenants noted that this beard was a true barometer of his disposition. When pleased, he stroked it lovingly; when displeased it stood straight out and was disregarded. When the news of the second inspection reached Captain Jim, he smiled and stroked his beard complacently. This was all the more strange for all the Regiment knew that Jim's irascible disposition, and his formation with the Inspector General at the first inspection, were responsible for this second visitation.

A review and inspection order came down from the Regiment and all awaited the arrival of the great man.

Promptly at nine the next morning, the Regiment formed on the parade in front of quarters and marched to the review field. The band played sweet music all the way. The regiment had its best foot forward. Everything was shined within an inch of its life and the old blue dress uniform made the formation colorful and inspiring.

The Pass-by in Review was reasonably good for an outfit just returned from three months in the field—with the glaring exception of I Company. This unit was having trouble getting from column into line and the comments of the file closers were lurid, but finally they made it.

Just before the line passed the Inspector General at the reviewing line, it simply went to pieces. There was no alignment; at *Eyes Right* soldiers peeked out from under the elbows of the files next in line; the step slowed down, and wave after wave swept the full length of the Company's fractional line.

Well out in front of the company, with head high and beard sharply protruding like a bayonet fixed to his chin, Captain Jim Bayle saluted proudly. His bearing and the awful appearance of the marching company were too much for the Inspector General. He completely discarded all pretense of dignity and shouted in loud and enraged tones "Captain Bayle, that Company marches like a god-damned flock of sheep."

Captain Bayle saluted in acknowledgment of the message and yelled back in even greater volume.

"Yep, We ain't much on marching, but we're hell on pickin' pecans!"

That did it. We never heard what took place in the Colonel's office when Captain Jim was called there, but the betting in the mess was that nothing would happen and nothing did.

The Regiment, in complete confidence, referred to I Company as the *Pecan Pickers* for years but never in the presence of Captain Jim, nor the Inspector General.

Innocence Rewarded

The sand blowing across the square cut Richard McCarthy like a knife and the young man, in apparent endeavor to save his once white, but now sadly begrimed white collar, hurriedly grasped at the troublesome thing and turned his back to the approaching small cyclone.

The day seemed unusually dark for a day in June and it seemed more than dark to McCarthy as he stood in line awaiting his turn to be examined physically by a short, taciturn, and very worried looking doctor.

The doctor had been sent down from San Antonio to this small south Texas town to determine the fate of some seventy odd draftees. There was not much warlike talk among the young huskies who stood in front of the small office and it struck the doctor that his presence there was about as welcome to the inhabitants as was the presence two years before of the District Court whose sessions had come to an untimely and violent end.

There was no sign of hostility in the attitude of the townspeople however, but it seemed that he was not going to be popular in that community and that was all.

The doctor, however, knew his duty and was seeing that it was properly done. He glanced up to see one McCarthy standing before him clad in the same clothing which he wore on the day he made the acquaintance of the world—and wearing in addition a broad and shamefaced grin. It needed no medical practitioner to see that McCarthy was about as perfect a specimen as this country of ours produced.

The doctor went carefully through the list of questions as propounded by the Army regulations and then went ahead to give the candidate the eye and ear tests. From the results, deducible from the answers of McCarthy, it seemed that the candidate could see the eye chart at twenty feet only with great difficulty. As for hearing the sound of a watch at arm's length, it was as a machine gun at twenty miles.

The doctor, with a slightly amused look, turned toward the window and gazed off into space, drumming lightly on the window sill as he looked though the dust storms.

"So," he muttered, "you are having trouble with your ears."

The candidate who was at the other side of the room, some forty feet away, promptly replied, "Yes, Sir, I reckon I done caught cold in 'em when I was nothing but a right small baby. I heard my mother say I did any way."

The doctor smiled again, and suddenly becoming all attention said, "Well, I declare, I do believe I see an Oriole way out there in the chaparral. This seems late in the year to see those birds here."

The candidate, catching at the chance of a brief respite from his physical exam, jumped excitedly to the window and looked out. He saw at a glance the bird at which the doctor had been looking and turning on the doctor with great sarcasm delivered himself of this opinion. "A party could sure tell, Doc, that you was raised in the city. That there bird you all are looking at is a Tanninger bird. It ain't no more robin than a jack rabbit."

The doctor turned savagely on the boy who had so easily fallen into his trap and said, "What did you mean by telling me you couldn't see clearly and that you were unable to hear? Don't you realize that your country is in danger and that if you and others like you manage through your falseness to evade the right of going to her assistance, our nation is bound to collapse and to get the fate that under the circumstances she would so richly deserve?"

The young man listened astounded, then gasped and the habitual grin reappeared. Then he remarked to the room in general "Hell, I don't know nothing about this soldier business and maybe there's others that do, and you know, Doc, it ain't like me to go for to crowd anybody out of a place, but there's just this about it. If ya'll think I'm afraid to go along, why I guess I'll just naturally have to go and do it."

He was accordingly certified as fit for military service, marked A1 and about two weeks later Private Richard McCarthy dropped from a freight train in San Antonio and, with a highly disinterested air, started for the camp on the outskirts of the town to comply with the written instructions which he carried along with three dollars in his dilapidated pocket book.

Private McCarthy bore himself well during his three months of training and went through the regular stages of becoming a soldier. He skipped nothing and added a short time in the guardhouse to his other experiences. He seemed, however, not enthused too much over his adopted career and his general intelligence told him that the final outcome of all the work that was being expended upon him by his noncoms and officers was for no other purpose than to fit him to kill a man or more if possible; to do it the right way and the right time; and to do it, if possible, without killing himself at the same time. This prospect never appealed to Private. McCarthy, but as he received plenty of exercise and plenty of food, and as the life seemed to him to be some sort of a game which everybody was playing at this particular time, he was not disposed to complain, but to get all the comfort and enjoyment out of it while the "getting was good" as he carefully put it.

He was rated as a First Class Private by an overbearing First Sergeant who seemed to be more exacting than any range boss known to the southwest; who for some unknown reason took an exceedingly active interest in even the most personal questions, which seemed to perpetually confront the privates of his company of infantry. He had been known to lend money at intervals, but never to anyone other than the most hard boiled of the NCO's and then only for an extremely limited time.

Having come from the regular service, it struck the members of this command that he must have been raised in most unusual surroundings, but when OD shirts and shoes began to disappear with surprising regularity from beneath bunks, the company decided that the Sergeant was right after all and that the world is made up a surprisingly great number of types of men and each began to pattern slowly after their martinet, and incidentally, began to look surprisingly like solid good, self reliant soldiers.

This progressed to such a degree that when a cruel and bloodthirsty Colonel of the regular Army posing for the time being as an Inspector General came to look them over and to decide as to whether they were fit for service abroad, went his way carrying with him a recommendation that they be sent over at once and even went so far as to ask for an assignment to command that particular Regiment.

His request for command was promptly refused by the Chief Clerk who reviewed it and who was at the time acting for the War Department, but as his recommendation went to another source it was promptly acted upon and the Regiment was started forthwith to the nearest port of embarkation, which rumor had it, was to be the famous port of Hoboken, New Jersey.

Private McCarthy having caught the contagious excitement of the moment was, for the nonce, drawn out of his usual self and expressed himself with great feeling on the German and all his products, and recalled to his companions the time when having become all lit up on German beer in the peaceful town of Waco he had been committed to jail after a short argument with a policeman by the name of Greenburg whom he now recalled to have addressed him with a strong German accent.

His memory was somewhat hazy on this point, but what he lacked in memory was more than balanced by his imaginative qualities and the story lost nothing in the telling.

"He showed me right then and there," vouchsafed Private McCarthy, "that you never can tell a damn thing about them Germans.

"He said that he was taking me to another place for to buy me a drink, but that bird dragged me straight to the police station. When he had dragged me to a police joint, he hit me on the bean with a night stick so hard that he just about sprained my ankles. He done that to me he did, and they ain't nobody can tell me that we won't have to round up them people and ride a herd guard on 'em for the rest of their natural lives."

In the solitude of his bunk that night, however, Private McCarthy thought of other things. He thought first of the submarines, which were roaming the Atlantic, and he had a mental picture of drifting about on the ocean clad in one of the life preservers so extensively advertised in the service papers. He then formed a mental picture of how he was going to feel going over the top following the First Sergeant, and what if that worthy were killed? There was then no alternative except to lead the charge straight at the enemy's machine guns, and machine guns were no slouches, as he knew from carefully watching them at range practice.

He then saw himself wounded and lying in the shell cratered no man's land as he had heard it carefully described by a British lecturer who had a friend who had once been in such a state. He pictured the horrible pain, the thirst that comes to the wounded man, the attempt to get back and the last dying effort, and in the midst of this last dream he went to sleep to enjoy the sleep that comes from an untroubled conscience and physical exhaustion.

When he awoke and turned out for reveille, however, he was unable to shake off the thoughts of the day before. He wondered that he had taken any interest in the game of war before. It now seemed to him to have become an unexpectedly personal thing and "Dammit, here I am like a jackrabbit and I cain't run," seemed to him to sum up the whole situation.

His mental condition did not, however, interfere with his efficiency as a soldier, as the First Sergeant as calm as the first days of May saw to it that he did the work of two or three men and the other NCO's taking their cue from the First Sergeant and from the Company Officers went coolly about checking the items of equipment and preparing their units for the long journey. This took some little time and by noon, a long line of train cars were backed up on the siding. The Regiment was duly entrained in thorough discomfort and the trip to Germany was begun.

The atmosphere of Private McCarthy's car soon took a decidedly blue tinge from countless cigarettes. The passengers, after having exhausted themselves from yelling from the car windows at the many girls on the platforms of the various stations, soon started a crap game and if General Pershing himself had been able to inspect the train he would have found great difficulty in distinguishing the journey from any one of a hundred like journeys made by all Regiments of the Army since the beginning of railway transportation.

Private McCarthy, however, quickly tired of his favorite game of craps, and was assisted in his determination to retire from it by a temporary lack of funds with which to continue, and a stern refusal on the part of the winners of his small account to even consider a loan of any kind. He then retired to a window and tried to picture the members of his squad; thoughtfully carrying his body back of the line to receive a final and proper internment. This thought cheered him considerably.

He thought of the First Sergeant, and he knew that worthy well enough not to fear that he would harbor any grudge and he could almost hear him saying, "Men, that was a damned good soldier man, and he was there with the punch when the punch was needed, but he sure was a wild man when he got his Irish going." That would be a great moment decided Private McCarthy, but then came the awful realization that he, the principal figure in the show, was supposed to be dead and that no amount of pride which might attend his internment was going to alter the fact that he had finished his job and would be planted securely in a hole. This changed his plans considerably and as he pondered over the whole affair, he sank again to the uttermost depths and again sought solace in slumber.

The detrainment was even more horrible than the entrainment, and after standing in line for an hour or more near the station at which the horrible detraininent had taken place, and listening to the publication by the Company Commander of thousands of orders affecting the possible embarkation, Private McCarthy was suddenly awakened from his reverie by a nudge on his left elbow by No. 2 of his squad who whispered, "Let's do it."

Private McCarthy was game to do anything and quickly followed No. 2 who had stepped two paces to the front, and with habitual precision,

Private. McCarthy placed his hand on his hip, dressed carefully up to No. 2 and waited. It was not until after the dismissal of the Company and an assignment to tents that Private McCarthy discovered that he had applied for and received a pass of twenty-four hours and would be at liberty to go wheresoever he wished provided that he was properly dressed and did not violate any of the ten thousand orders issued upon the subject of visiting towns.

Lost Over

This is a story about the old Regular Army and its environment in which I was brought up as a small boy. In those days a Non-Commissioned Officer (Corporals, Sergeants, etc) were the backbone of the Army. They knew all of the "tricks of the trade" which they developed and used to keep their Commanders in good standing and themselves out of trouble.

The heroes in the following two stories are the "non coms" who were typical of their breed in the Army of that day.

Lost Over

If I were called upon to classify officers of the Army, I might start by putting them roughly into one or more of the following three classes:

1. Those who are always around when something happens;

2. Those to whom something always seems to happen;

3. Those who are neutrals, that is, are in neither class 1 nor 2.

Fortunately no officer is saddled with such classification which is now done by a Board headed by a civilian with an outstanding degree.

For my money, Captain Charles Wright Beery of the artillery could have well claimed to be the original member of both classes one and two.

He was originally commissioned in the Coast Artillery Corps, but at the outbreak of World War I, in an outburst of patriotism and with a desire to see some action, had immediately transferred to the Field Artillery and to a light gun unit, at that.

In this, he was more than lucky for there was not much action for heavy artillery; in fact, the only really heavy stuff to appear on the front in American hands was commanded by a Rear Admiral of the Navy—why, I never knew.

Captain Beery was one of these wiry, red-headed chaps whose curiosity was always uppermost. He wound up with a motorized unit of medium howitzers and did excellent work with them. He tried to learn French and then German, but gave it up as too much to add to an artilleryman's duties. The point is, that he was always active. There was some question about his exercise of good judgment in his activity, but that was only in the minds of his seniors—his juniors knew, but kept their knowledge to themselves.

When the war ended, he was in the Army which marched to the Rhine. Not that his unit saw much of him, for he felt that he should be up in front with the leaders and since there was quite a number of cars exactly like his own, he got by.

The First Division had not been long on the Rhine when General Summerall, whose pride in its accomplishments was great and well justified, decided that the Division should be paraded and reviewed in honor of several of its officers who had been cited in orders. He would bestow the medals. There were quite a few of them and it would take more than the usual time allotted for such a formation. More than that, he was a stickler for readiness for immediate field service and directed his staff to include in the order for the review the directive that "All units will have a meal in preparation in their rolling kitchens."

The Division had had ample time to get its men and equipment into immaculate condition.

Everything was freshly painted; all harness was clean and oiled; trace chains were painted; all motors were freshly cleaned; and all brass shiny; and finally, all men were in their best uniforms.

They made a sight to gladden a soldier's heart.

Captain Beery's battery was not lacking in any of these things. There was no doubt in his mind that be compared favorably with any other battery-motor or horse drawn in the whole Division.

It was not until they had marched to the review field and were waiting for formation to start that Captain Beery discovered, to his great unease that he had overlooked the rolling kitchen and the "meal in preparation" part.

He was really downcast. The cooks in the adjoining batteries were stocking their kitchens with a reassuring cloud of smoke arising and the smell of rations was beginning to make itself evident.

He called his First Sergeant, the universal source of supporting strength to a Battery Commander. He explained his situation and shouldered the blame for it. "I guess I didn't read the order the way it was written. There's nothing to be done about it now, I guess."

But the First Sergeant was a resourceful soldier of some years of service and without any inhibitions when it came to his battery. "Don't worry, Sir," he countered, "I think that we can get through all right without anybody seeing that our rolling kitchens aren't preparing a meal. I'll go over to one of those horse drawn units there, and borrow a piece of bailing wire. They're bound to have some, and I'll pour some engine oil on a piece of waste and put it down the chimney of the rolling kitchen. We'll make more damn smoke than any of these units when we pass in review and General Summerall will never know."

Captain Beery was delighted with the idea. He patted the First Sergeant on the shoulder. "John, you've done it again. I won't forget it."

The Sergeant went for the nearest horse drawn unit and returned with the wire.

Captain Beery went down to give a last minute appeal to the cannoneers and the tractor drivers.

"You cannoneers, don't forget that General Summerall is an artilleryman himself. There will be no slouching on the carriages. Sit erect, when you pass in review. Keep your arms folded and up off your chests. And that applies to all the assistant tractor drivers, too. And you drivers, you drive and keep your minds on your work. Keep your distances and intervals."

He continued in this vein and went back to his post certain that aside from the rolling kitchen arrangements, he had overlooked nothing.

The pass-by under the eyes of the reviewing officer was all that could be desired. General Summerall seemed pleased by the driving and the alignment, but Captain Beery from his car in front of the center of his battery was suddenly struck by the concentrated and somewhat puzzled look on the face of the reviewing officer after the battery had passed.

He kept peering after Beery's battery and finally turned to the line of orderlies in rear of his staff and beckoned one up to him.

They talked a minute and the orderly saluted and mounted his horse. He took up a fast gallop and rode opposite Captain Beery's car.

"General Summerall," be roared, "says for you to get them asbestos tailed cooks off that damn hot cook stove."

Captain Beery looked back. There sat the cooks at attention their arms stiffly folded and horizontal on the top of the rolling kitchen from which a most *satisfactory* smoke was issuing. There was nothing to be done.

He knew that General Summerall and his Regimental Commander would do it for him.

I think that was about 1923 or 1924 that the real blight hit the commissioned side of the Army. This was the year when the morale of the Regular Army hit an all time low for orders came from Washington directing the release by name of many officers whose performance in combat and otherwise had been good, but who had some dereliction of duty or breach of discipline on their records and they were ordered to be separated from the service.

Contrary to the general belief of our Nation, the morale of a unit is a true reflection of the morale of its officers, and consequently there was not much of it left.

It was not unusual for an officer reporting at a new station to be handed an order separating him from the service—a rough greeting indeed.

The cut in funds, which caused this affair, hit the enlisted strength hard. Many posts were placed upon a care-taking basis with just enough men to keep the armament from deteriorating, and most of the units were grouped around the service schools to act as demonstration units.

Aside from these units, in the infantry, there were barely enough men in the companies to allow the Sergeants, Corporals and others who normally formed as the file closers to hide behind. In this period every effort was being made to keep military skills from joining the other lost arts.

Based on an equality of population of military age, the United States Army termed the Zone of the Interior, had been divided into nine Corps Areas (each planned to mobilize a Corps when necessary to meet a major emergency) with a Commanding General and staff; reporting directly to the War Department.

In spite of the terribly reduced strength of the Army, these Commanding Generals still had the duty of inspecting the units within their Corps Areas and keeping them up to standard in their training.

Captain Charles Wright Beery, now a Colonel, was in command of Fort Moultrie, at the entrance to Charleston Harbor; and since the post was on a care-taking basis, with a small detachment of some twenty men to keep the artillery with their electric systems, the communications with the Corps Area, the ammunition and the fire control instruments all in efficiently operating condition, the duties of the Commanding Officer were not too demanding.

Colonel Beery knew that he was not supposed to train gun crews, nor to shoot. His job centered around maintenance. So, when it came time for the annual tactical inspections, he felt no qualms; instead he was about to congratulate himself on not having to risk such inspection at such an inauspicious time when a poor efficiency report might result in his being put on the list of those on their way out of the Army.

He was rudely awakened from this happy dream of exemption by an order from his Corps Area Commander to the effect that he would be given a tactical inspection within the next month and that it would consist principally in his firing for record a battery of 12-inch guns. The order went onto assure him that the mission of his small detachment there was well understood to be maintenance and not training, but such firing would show better than any other form of inspection the "readiness for action and the efficiency of the maintenance of the armament with all its communications."

Back at Corps Area Headquarters in Atlanta, a Board was appointed to conduct the inspection.

Most of the Board was from the Office of the Coast Artillery District Commander. Of course, the Chief of Ordnance of the Corps was on it; and the Chief Armament Machinist of the Corps, a most important addition.

This latter gentleman was an extraordinary individual. In addition to being a most efficient Armament Machinist, he utilized his Sundays and holidays in his second profession, which was that of a Pastor of several small churches in the vicinity of the post churches which, had no assigned pastors. He was widely known and respected as a man of great piety. His thick chested figure was always around when artillery was involved in its practice, and he had been known to administer mild reprimands to Chiefs of Section and gunners when under stress they had profanely expressed their opinions.

Colonel Beery met the Board at their train and took them at once to the battery selected. To its satisfaction, the members found a gun crew waiting and everything in place for the firing.

It had been no small matter to produce this condition. There had to be an arrangement with the Coast Guard to inspect the target area; warnings had been published to all shipping and repeated for a period; local fishermen and boat owners had had to be apprised of the danger areas. In addition to all this, Colonel Beery had had to train his maintenance party to function as members of a gun crew.

They were all old soldiers with service in several artillery units, so that part of it was not too difficult, and the Board, after checking on all the necessary precautions for the firing, put the improvised gun crew through a drill and found to their great satisfaction that all members, firing battery, spotters, plotters, observers and ammunition handlers knew their business.

Colonel Beery went nervously from one group of inspectors to another, and the Armament Machinist tried to relax him a little by telling the Senior Officer of the Board that so far as he could see, the battery was in fine shape for firing.

Finally, all the members having finished each his particular part, the Senior Officer turned to Colonel Beery and gave the long awaited command, "You may commence firing when your target is in position." All the members stared through their glasses at the tugboat towing a target just about on the horizon.

The observers gave their azimuths to the plotters; the plotters located the target and computed its azimuth for the guns; the Colonel translated the data into terms of ammunition—of powder and projectile—and in a very short time a voice came up from the pit, "Battery ready."

"Fire," commanded the Colonel and all the Board members raised their glasses to spot the shot whose splash should appear somewhere in the vicinity of the target. The Observers in the crew were scanning the whole sea front.

Silence.

No one had any idea of where the round had fallen.

"Lost," reported observer #1

"Lost," reported observer #2

"Lost, over," reported the Colonel, turning to the senior member. "Shall I fire another, Sir?"

The Senior Member nodded, but some slight disturbance in the pit turned them all towards the battery. The Chief Armament Machinist had taken off his shirt, and, surrounded by members of the gun crew, was joining them in a desperate effort to open the breech block.

The First Sergeant of the detachment now approached the group around the gun's breech. He was purposefully grasping a sixteen pound hammer and the members clearly heard his enraged plea to the armament machinist, "Stand outta the way, Fred, and gimme a shot at the son-of-a-bitch."

"No, Sergeant," this in shocked tones, "you must never strike a breech block handle with a metal hammer. Get me my kit bag and I'll have her open in a minute. I need a little raw hide hammer I use for this very thing."

As the sun got higher, the heat in the pit became almost unbearable. The Board waited with what patience they could muster and discussed opinions as to where the first and only round had landed. The consensus was that it was well "over the hill" and since it probably was outside safety limits, everyone was in jeopardy until it was certain that no luckless ship had wandered in to its path.

The Chief Armament Machinist sweating in every pore, was still trying with his rawhide hammer. Gently and with assurance, he stroked the breech block handle taking care not to continue striking in one place, so as not to dent it. As the heat grew more intense in the pit, his strokes became more determined and approached desperation. Still he was coolly appraising the job and was calmness itself

The First Sergeant could be heard, trying to persuade the Armament Machinist to let him take just one swing with the sixteen-pound hammer. This was steadily refused.

Then, the Machinist went again to his kit and brought a heavier copper hammer. The sweat was running in a stream down his bare back. He started with a certain amount of restraint, with fairly gentle strokes, well distributed along the handle; but under the insistence of the gun crew, that they were in danger of sunstroke, his efforts became more forceful; and shortly he was raining blows with all his strength.

The Chief of Ordnance became uneasy and paced slowly up and down along the parapet. This dislodged some sand, which fell gently on the sweaty backs of the gun crew huddled in a group below and brought forth comments unfavorable to everything in the vicinity.

And then the voice of the Machinist made itself heard over the confusion in the pit. "This is the worst (grunt) jam (grunt) I have seen in twenty years as a (grunt) as a Armament Machinist." The mood of the gun crew changed instantly and their smiles showed their appreciation of the lapse on the part of the Machinist, that pious man.

But he continued to work with his copper hammer. Still, there was no perceptible movement on the part of the obdurate block. None of the artillerymen on the Board had any suggestions. They all knew that when a breech block decided not to open, it is in the same class as an obstinate safe, which becomes impregnable to any legal manner of assault.

The Armament Machinist wiped his wet face on his undershirt. It was evident that he had passed the limit of endurance for humans; he had hit the block handle with everything prescribed in the handbook; he had even hammered on the face of the block from the muzzle of the piece with a rammer, but with no result. It was nearing lunch hour.

Under the prodding of the gun crew, he suddenly became a screaming maniac. "Gimme that heavy hammer," he yelled at the First Sergeant, "I'll show this damned gun what's what."

"Get outa the way, Fred, I'll hit her myself: You ought'na on account your rating."

"Rating, hell!" gritting his teeth "Gimme that hammer, I'll show this goddamn old bitch who's boss around here." He swung once, twice, three times.

The only result was that the Chief of Ordnance dashed down into the pit. He took the Chief Machinist by the shoulder and led him away.

"Suspend this practice," he directed "until we can determine what is the matter here." When Col. Beery hesitated and glanced appealingly at the Senior Board Member, he added, "It is unsafe to fire again and I assume complete responsibility." That ended it for the morning.

That afternoon the Board returned to Headquarters leaving the Chief of Ordnance and the Machinist to open the block and to hold a postmortem. They passed the Chief Machinist on the way to the station. He was very red in the face and was muttering to himself as he sat in his little car in front of the Ordnance Office. They respected his embarrassment and did not speak to him as they passed.

Inside the mess hall, where the gun crew was having lunch, there was much merry making and loud expressions of appreciation for the show put on by the Armament Machinist. There were also fond hopes that maybe the lost round had busted up one of the fishermen whom the crew didn't like.

Gangster

Without exception the gangsters I have known have been a rather filthy and cowardly lot. Anyone who has spent his life in the Army knows the type well enough from years back; when the outside going got rough, the Army was sought as a refuge for those with a "passion for anonymity." Of course, the finger print identification spelled the end of that.

When in World War II, the 94th Division, which I then commanded, made its way from the Saar to the Rhine, and from there to Dusseldorf, I remembered that in World War I we had found all the drugstores stripped of narcotics. In spite of all we could do, we were never able to locate the gang who was doing the stripping. In fact, we never knew whether they were American, French, British, or German. This time I would watch out for that particular situation.

Since we had taken many towns and cities, we knew very well how to do it and I, with my aide, went in with the Advance Guard and each time, made straight for the drug stores.

Without exception, the narcotics were gone and I came to the conclusion that the gang was in the German Army—not in ours.

Quite accidentally, I became a sought-for gangster myself once.

It happened when I was an instructor in a School for Machine Gunners in Harlington, Texas.

Three of us had written a book on those weapons and we constituted the faculty of the school.

Those machine gun units on the Texas border came to us regularly and stayed a couple of weeks, while we gave them a very practical course in the several types of machine guns with which our Army was at that time equipped.

Our camps were on the edge of an *arroyo* along in front of which a nice stream flowed, and since the country was right for it, and there were no dwellings for miles, we fired from about eight in the morning until four in the afternoon.

When we had a gun fail by reason of a major part which had to be replaced, we took it up to the Ordnance Depot and fired to check the repair, just outside the town and along the main road.

We were on such a job one spring morning. Captain (later Maj. Gen. Hatcher) was in the front seat of the Dodge Open car, which we had borrowed from the Ordnance Officer without his knowledge, while I, with the machine gun, was holding down the back seat. It was a light gun of the Hotchkiss type and the feed strip with full ammunition load, stuck straight out from the breech end. The deadly nature of the weapon was unmistakable. Both Hatcher and I were clad in grease spotted overalls.

Along the dusty road stood one of the roughest looking characters we had seen in many a day. The morning promised to be hot and Hatcher with his usual good nature, stopped the car and threw open the front door.

"Want a ride?" he smiled.

"Yeah."

I stuck my machine gun out over the side.

"Get in," I said "and sit there in front."

He got in and we went silently up the road at the fastest speed the old Dodge would make. After a few miles, Hatcher asked, "Where do you want to get out?"

The character swallowed hard. "Fer Chris sake, any place. Lemme off right here." The relief in his voice was evident. We dropped him off and went on to do our job.

On the way back, we were passed by first the Sheriff going great guns, then by two Rangers. All of them knew us and waved at us quite merrily.

Upon our arrival at the Ordnance Depot, the Ordnance Officer regarded us with a certain amount of suspicion. "You can go right down to your damned school," he growled, "and inventory every damned gun in the hands of your troops units and in your school magazines."

"What's the matter?"

"There are a couple of gangsters riding around in a car with no number on it and they are shooting up the villages with a machine gun. Where you been?"

"Up towards Mercedes," said Hatcher, and tossed a coat over the machine gun on the floor in back.

The Ordnance Officer loaned us his car to go back to the school and we kept it there for a day or two to protect the Ordnance Officer.

Tramp

It is not enough to be able to produce the most advanced type weapons. There still remains the task of training the average citizen to use them properly and to maintain them in operating condition.

This fact has been driven home to more than one nation, and was the reason for the great machine gun controversy, which raged in this country in 1914.

Machine guns were an essentially American invention. Gatling made the first practicable one; Maxim left the ideas of Gatling behind and made the first portable one; Browning had a different set of ideas and showed up at Colt's in Hartford with one embodying a new principle; and Lewis adapted these new ideas to a lighter and consequently more terrible type of gun.

In 1914, Lewis had sold his gun to the British after having tried unsuccessfully to sell it to the United States. In this, he followed in the footsteps of Maxim.

In each case, the Congress had refused to appropriate funds for the purchase. In looking back over the record, it seems fairly clear that the machine gun experts in the Congress of that day did not do well with their work.

Villa's stupid raid on Columbus, New Mexico brought matters to a head. In that raid, the guns of LT Lucas (afterward Gen. Lucas of Anzio fame), manned by such men as he could find to pad out a few of his machine gun troops for action. While they had been in action, they had been ineffective and an investigation of the affair convinced the members of Congress that our program needed a lot of overhauling. The Chief of Ordnance was held to be blameworthy and eventually was replaced.

The technical services held that the fault lay not in the gun, but in the state of instruction of the troops. Out of that grew the creation of a school for their instruction located close to the center of gravity of the Army, which at that time was mainly concentrated on the Mexican border.

Captain (Maj. Gen., later) Hatcher rescued me from the hands of the 26th Infantry and made me his assistant in the set-up of the school; later

LT W. Doe and OP Wilhelm were added and the school settled down to the job of instruction.

We worked hard and made great progress. Hatcher made the job an enjoyable one and it was always interesting for we had a new unit in for instruction weekly and certainly the interest in the guns and in their possibilities rose rapidly. We were greatly helped by the reports of their fantastic deadlines, which came from the overseas areas where the Germans were driving the Allies back from Mons.

The site of the school was ideal for our purposes. In front of the low bluff on which such canvas shelter as we needed was set up, flowed a little river across which we fired from a series of trenches. These were so near as we could construct them, of the type in use in Belgium and France, and served the double purpose of keeping gun squads from firing into each other, and showing the application of the guns to positions in trench warfare.

As our skill with the guns increased, Hatcher evolved an idea of competition designed to "keep us up against the bit." Every morning, before the arrival of the troops for training, each of us took a gun of his own selection and set up in it the hardest and most irreducible jam he could think of.

We had many different types of guns there and it was easy to select a favorite for this kind of sport. Guns which were made to be mounted in tripods were avoided, if possible, for we became accustomed to working so fast that if one had to stop to set up a tripod, he was very likely to come out last. Having set up the malfunction, we exchanged guns and rushed for the firing line. There we were to fire fifty rounds and the one who was last in firing his quota was to buy beer for the four of us that night.

The area to our front where we fired was uninhabited for many miles. The only watch we had to keep was of the railroad, which skirted the edge of our range. It was the main line leading to Brownsville. The country was arid and flat and we could see the trains for miles before they arrived.

One morning in late spring, we had gathered for the exchange of guns and Hatcher had drawn an old Maxim. This gun when filled with water weighed some fifty odd pounds and was a tripod mounted affair. Since he was to fire only fifty rounds, he omitted the filling of the water jacket.

At the command "GO" we raced for the firing line, and intent on getting the guns firing, each of us tried to locate the difficulty in his weapon.

Hatcher was the speediest of all. He didn't try to set up a tripod, simply sat down, rested the gun in his lap and across his leg, yanked the roller handle, thereby loading the gun and without looking through the sights, fired his first burst on his fifty rounds, down into the little river below.

There was a wild yell from the direction of the river and for the first time, we looked down on the terrain over which we were firing.

Behind a large bush on the flit side of the stream, a naked figure rose and ran for the railroad bank. He scrambled up the cindery bank. Apparently, he had been washing his clothes in the stream, for hanging on the bush in the sun, was a full set of underclothing.

We yelled "Stop, come back!" but no reaction. By this time he had up a full head of steam and was making time down the railroad in the general direction of Brownsville. We knew that the arrival of fifty rounds of service ammunition in the river directly in front of him had scared the hell out of him, so we gave up yelling and watched him go.

He ran and ran until he looked just a few inches high on the horizon.

I have always wondered what could have become of a naked man in Texas. We never heard.

The Irish Dilemma

When I was a cadet at the United States Military Academy, the Superintendent of the institution was General Thomas Barry. I still think that apart from General Pershing, he was about the most military figure and one of the handsomest men I have ever known.

It became my fate to be selected to sing a song at one of those entertainments held at West Point on the Hundredth Day before graduation; and this song had a somewhat scurrilous application to the tactical officer of my company.

While I was singing, I wondered how the Superintendent was taking it and looked to his box, the closest to the stage. He was in gales of laughter and I was quite content for I had had visions of walking tours on the cadet area throughout the rest of the Academic year.

I did not realize that this song marked me ineradicably by name in the mind of the Superintendent and that this flattering recollection would rise up to smite me, at intervals, throughout the remaining active years of General Barry's service.

Upon graduation, I had expressed my preference of service as Alaska and had all my uniforms made to fit that very cold climate. I can still remember with a felling of elation how my very expensive overcoat—with a hood, no less—looked. All my other clothes were made to correspond. You can get some idea of my predicament when my orders finally emerged sending me for duty in Panama.

That was a real lesson to me, but I apparently did not profit by it, for when it came time for me to express my preference for station upon termination of my tour in Panama, I became very cautious about telling anyone where I wanted to go.

By sweet talking the medical officers into it, and after having had two bouts with dengue and malaria fevers, I induced the most venturesome one of them to write a letter to the Adjutant General telling him and the whole world that I was not only a chronic sufferer from malaria, but that I was a carrier. This should insure me a northern station.

All the Regular Army was at that time on the Texas border and I hoped not, repeat not, to join them there.

Again. Imagine my predicament when my orders came out sending me, this time, to Harbinger, Texas.

But, it was in Panama that General Barry first stumbled upon me after I left the Academy.

It happened that I was Officer of the Day and after having made the required inspections of the guard, mounted, I had tied my horse to the hitch rack in front of Headquarters and just before reveille, sat at a desk there, thoroughly immersed in a nickel novel I had borrowed from the Sergeant of the Guard at the Guard House. I checked the presence of the buglers to sound reveille and relaxed.

Shortly after reveille sounded, I heard some one come into the building, but paid little attention for I thought that it might be one of the Sergeants-Major with something to do before the CO arrived. The footsteps seemed to have stopped at my desk and the never-to-be forgotten voice of General Barry said, "Well, are you going to get on your feet or not?"

Before I could recover, and after I had scrambled to attention, "Mr. Malony," he said, "where the hell are your spurs? There on that inkstand?"

I admitted it.

"And whose horse is that out there walking in his bridle?"

"Mine, Sir."

"Well, get out there and straighten him out."

"Yes, Sir," and I fled to do his bidding.

But I didn't stop with the horse; I ran for the nearest outside phone and called the Adjutant, the Commanding Officer, the Battalion Commanders and left strict orders with the switchboard operator to keep on calling and to inform everyone that the Commanding Officer of the Eastern Department was in the Post and to waste no time in getting to their units.

I returned to the Headquarters.

"Where is everybody?" inquired the General. I reminded him that reveille had just gone and that they were undoubtedly on their way to breakfast.

I sent my orderly for the General's.

When he had finished it, he felt better and said to me, "Have you been singing lately?" I modestly denied it. He started to say something, but changed his mind as the Adjutant put in an appearance.

The Adjutant immediately became very active. "Good morning, Sir," he said quite cheerfully. "Won't you come into the office?" He found time to say to me "Go home, Mr. Malony, change your clothes and report back to General Barry as his aide-de-camp while he is here."

I left very reluctantly, for it looked like an active day among the field officers and I did not want to miss anything. I galloped home, put on my best khaki and my boots and hurried back.

By that time, things were moving all over. I saw my comrade Lieutenants hurrying to their units; troops were forming, and the Commanding Officer hurried into his office.

From the expression on the face of the Adjutant, I gathered that the day had not started as he might have wished it to and I was sorry to have missed the interview. They were two of a kind. Determined not to miss any more of this glorious devastation, I hastened to knock on the CO's door and to report as General Barry's aide. He simply nodded, returned my most military salute and told me to wait outside.

Officers and Sergeants Major came and went in absolute silence. They tiptoed by the door. I sat in solitary splendor pointing mysteriously at the CO's door from which loud sounds all made by General Barry were emergent.

Suddenly the door opened. General Barry motioned to me. "Come in here," he ordered abruptly.

"How long have you been with this regiment, Mr. Malony?"

Now was my opportunity to do something nice for the CO "Two years, Sir."

"Have you completed your garrison school?"

"Yes, Sir."

"Have you been shown, and have you studied, some secret maps sent down here?" Ah! This was the hooker. He was going to get someone for a security violation. It was bound to be the CO. Not through the Iron Duke. Not on my testimony. "No, Sir," I replied proudly.

He turned fiercely upon the CO. "There. That settles it. Here is an officer of your command who has been with you two years and he has never heard of those maps. I sent them down here to be studied and not to be kept in a damned safe."

My mistake, but maybe I could make a recovery. "I was gone two months on leave," I said firmly. "They might have had them in school during my absence."

"Get the hell out of here," he roared, and I got.

So, in the year 1917, five years later, when I came aboard a transport in Liverpool bound back to the States after a tour with the flu in Queen Alexandra's Hospital in London, I was not at all overjoyed to see General Barry looking down from the top deck. I knew that he saw and recognized me. I was a little bit shy of baggage for you may remember that in World War I, the hospital employees and the litter carriers were somewhat careless about clothing and currency on the bodies of their wards and many a man arrived in the hospital picked as clean as a chicken. This was particularly true of such wounded as passed through French hands.

I had been given a pleasant mission of chaperoning two very friendly Britishers who were returning with us to the States to join in the work in progress then on the so-called Liberty Motor. This represented a pooling of all the motor manufacturers' knowledge and was popularly supposed to be designed to be used in airplanes, trucks, passenger cars, etc.

I suppose also that it was edible and could remove spots from uniforms—at least in its original concept.

Commander Briggs was the senior of the party. I had lately been promoted from Major to Lieutenant Colonel. Briggs and I amused ourselves by telling Leftenant Philipot about the peculiarities of the United States and its people. I think that we about had him convinced that we could put in a good weekend with bison hunting out Van Cortland Parkway.

For the first day, things went very well and that evening the end of a beautifully clear cold day, we were standing well out off Ireland and I and my two charges came on deck to take a little exercise preliminary to a cocktail. They made us both tipsy, for I was fresh from the hospital and Briggs was lately escaped from a prison camp. We saw General Barry and his staff standing at the stern, fixedly regarding Ireland, fast disappearing astern. A crowd around one man is an irresistible attraction and we sauntered along to join it.

General Barry was making quite an oration.

"Look there," he mused, "look at that little spot there and think of the people it has produced—the influence that that little island has had on human culture! The judges, the jurists, the religious leaders, the soldiers, the sailors, the administrators."

He stopped there, for we all at the same time, thought of the way the Irish were raising Cain with the English troops in their country.

The General continued, "They have left their marks in practically every country in the world and theirs has been a great gift to all with whom they have come in contact. But, Ireland," he paused, "is in a bad way now and I can't help wondering what would do her the most good."

I was horrified at the sight of my charge the Leftenant Commander who stepped blithely to the center of the circle and said slowly and quite distinctly, "Why *I* think that a tidal wave about forty feet high and lasting about three days should do the trick."

Here I made the great error of laughing and from the glance I got from General Barry I realized that only my name stood between me and maybe death itself.

He couldn't hit a man named Malony for laughing at his own antecedents without considerable prejudice. Now, could he?

Portrait of a Bretonne

> This is a true story about an iron willed old woman who demonstrated the indomitable strength that showed the true spirit of a people, a trait lacking in so many of us today.

Portrait of a Bretonne

In September of 1944, one of our Corps was systematically pounding Brest to pieces while the rest of our forces were yet, in full cry, hard upon the heels of the Germans. Our Division had been hurried up to relieve first an Armored Division and later, in addition, an Infantry Division. Both had been requested by General Patton for use in his pursuit and both were eager to be gone from the already forgotten front on Brittany.

These quick changes in orders and missions were each a hurry up! This was an "emergency order," gave our "standard order of procedure," commonly known in the Army as an SOP, a good work out.

About the middle of the month, I found myself on the road with a portion of the Division, headed for a beautiful little Breton city, which I had selected to be my new Headquarters. The early fall rains had begun; the country was sodden, but the coolness of fall was in the air; it brought with it a grave warning of icy battlefields, snowy bivouacs and frosty marches yet to come.

By the time I arrived there it was quite dark and my Headquarters Commandant met me with a guide at the entrance to the town. He conducted me straight to the Division Headquarters Mess, which, having preceded my column, had arrived in early afternoon and was set up and functioning. I did full justice to a good supper.

Of course, the town was blacked out. German aircraft was audible overhead even then, but the night was damp, cloudy and moonless—we furnished no targets. After supper we stood in the dark courtyard until our eyes became adjusted, then the Headquarters Commandant undertook to guide me on to my billet in which my meager personal effects bag had already been placed. It wasn't far, just a few doors down the street.

My guide kept feeling the doors with his fingers as we stumbled along, explaining as he did so, that there was a row of bullet holes across the front of mine, which made it easy to identify on dark nights. This he said was the sole evidence of prior occupancy by the Germans.

He knocked on the door, but there was no sound inside. He knocked again. The door was gently opened and I caught a fleeting glimpse of the form of an elderly French woman scurrying rapidly down the hall. The speed she made and the almost complete noiselessness of her departure were impressive.

"Mousie," I said to the Headquarters Commandant, "bids us enter."

"She is quiet," he replied, "and with damn good reason. She has had a German staff quarters on her for two years. They forbade her to speak above a whisper."

I was very busy for the next few days. Taking over a sector from troops in contact with an enemy requires considerable concentration and induces some preoccupation. If I saw my hostess at all, I don't remember it.

When things shook down a bit, and all the units were in place and in contact, the weather cleared and I became more conscious of the things going on around me. Then, I kept seeing "Mousie." She scuttled into the one room she reserved for herself every time I approached. As the days wore on, she frequently opened the door before I could knock and I realized that she was watching for my return. Her eager high-pitched whisper startled me more than if she had yelled at the top of her lungs "*Bon soir, M'sieu*."

"*Bon soir Mademoiselle, vous ailez bien?*"

Again a harsh whisper "*Bien, M'sieu*", and she had gone.

By the end of the second week she was speaking aloud. She had lively brown eyes set deep in a gaunt passive face. I estimated her age as pushing seventy, but she wore her years with dignity and might have been much younger. Her extreme shyness kept her silent when I knew she simply ached to speak. I was a little taken aback to find that she spoke English almost without accent.

All fear of us, if she had felt any from the beginning, seemed to have vanished. It was her evident desire to talk, but in her anxiety to be pleasant she frequently slipped back into that haunting, high-pitched, urgent whisper. I can shut my eyes and see her—sharp faced, anxious, her decent black dress, her shabby wooden-soled shoes, and her *pull-ovaire* sweater, poised like a prairie dog in front of his hole, ready to vanish into her room.

My aide-de-camp lived on the first floor, while I lived on the second. His French was perfect; mine didn't exist. He was not only my aide; he was my interpreter and my friend. Every human being who knew him had trusted him instinctively and *Mademoiselle* was no exception.

I was not too startled, when upon letting myself in one evening, to hear voices coming from *Mademoiselle*'s room—I recognized my aide's laugh and *Mademoiselle*'s voice, quite relaxed now, and burbling volleys of French with great energy and a high muzzle velocity. *Mademoiselle*, I thought, was recovering.

Then came Thanksgiving. Things had gone very well with the Division. Successful local attacks on our long front had netted us a fair number of prisoners. The junior leadership was becoming sound and skillful. We were polishing off two hard years of training in the States with a postgraduate course in small unit combat. I was proud of my units.

One of our Cavalry patrols south of Loire had brought in some champagne, which the Germans, with rare consideration, had labeled, *Not to be sold. Reserved for the Wehrmacht.* This made it a legitimate prize of war, and definitely removed it from the category of French property. The patrol turned over a few bottles to the Chief of Staff who invited the remainder of the staff and me to his room to enjoy it, and to celebrate Thanksgiving.

"How about *Mademoiselle* too?" I asked.

"Bring her along," he smiled. I so instructed my aide. I arrived late. The party assembled before me. When I entered, a *Mademoiselle* considerably changed from the one I thought I knew, sat on a sofa flanked on either side by a smiling member of my staff. Completely relaxed against the arm of the sofa, her knees crossed one over the other she displayed a scrawny, but serviceably sound leg.

She was quietly smoking an American cigarette which she, with a graceful swoop of her left hand removed from time to time, while in her right hand she held very purposefully indeed the remains of a Scotch highball. She smiled at me disclosing a jagged tooth line.

"We are awaiting you, *Mon General*," she said.

"But the champagne, *Mademoiselle?* These wicked officers of mine are plying you with whiskey. Of a truth, a strong and violent American drink."

Mademoiselle smiled at me pityingly. "I know well this *wheeskey* and I like eet. We but await your arrival for the champagne."

The Chief of Staff hastened to bring the champagne. *Mademoiselle* tossed off the remains of the highball and accepted her new glass with a sigh of appreciation. Again she relaxed on the sofa. The dimmed light of a dangling electric bulb, outlined *Mademoiselle's* bony features. Shadows cast by the intersecting planes on her face emphasized the rugged strength there. She raised her glass high and was obviously content. We all drank to France and America and to the confusion of our enemies.

Mademoiselle sat back in great satisfaction and addressed herself to my aide. The staff turned, as always, to divisional affairs. The aide who had anxiously been awaiting a chance to speak, turned to me.

"General," he said, "*Mademoiselle* has asked me to tell everyone here, especially the Chief of Staff, that she is very happy that you have allowed her to come here tonight to drink champagne. For just one year ago tonight, she said, she sat here on this same sofa, but between two German staff officers who tried to frighten her into drinking with them. She refused and they were pretty rough with her. She told them that she had no objection to drinking champagne and as a matter of fact she hoped and believed that a year from then she would be drinking champagne here, but instead of being seated between two officers of the German General Staff, she would be seated between two Americans.

'Then,' she told them, 'I shall be very happy.' So now she is grateful for being invited; for you have made her prophesy come true."

"But why didn't *Mademoiselle* tell us this herself?" I asked.

There ensued a few spirited passages between my aide and *Mademoiselle*, who sighed deeply.

"It is the whiskey, *Mon General*. Of a truth you were right about it. My English has now forsaken me."

The Division was so scattered over the tremendous frontage, which we were occupying, that to visit the principal units of the Division by motor required the greater part of a week. We habitually shortened our travel time by using Cub planes, but now the flying weather had become uncertain. The country was flat, damp, windswept, and bleak. It was no longer new to us. The FF1 was helping our units more and more effectively; but these topics palled during the following day when, accompanied by my aide, I started to make a swing through the Division. The talk sputtered and died until I mentioned *Mademoiselle*.

"You ought to be ashamed," I said, "She is a harmless shy old lady who at heart is still scared to death of us. She has tried in every way to propitiate us, and you youngsters are amusing yourselves teaching the old girl to drink whiskey and smoke cigarettes. Probably you have corrupted her English. You're making fun of her and she'll be damned humiliated when she finds out."

"No, Sir," he answered slowly "we've not been making fun of her—and if you have Mamselle sized up as being a nice old lady who doesn't know what gives around her you are due for some surprises yourself.

"Would you believe that she steamed open letters which she stole from the mail of German officers quartered upon her and copied important parts for the Resistance leaders?

"Would you put it beyond her to have made copies of all official orders left by the Berlin Courier for the German General in his quarters and have done it so skillfully that he, nor anyone else, ever found it out?

"Would you believe that she kept a diary, a list of collaborators with witnesses in this vicinity and has denounced many and that they are for the greater part in concentration camps now?

"Would you believe that when the Germans left hurriedly ahead of our troops, she ran out in the street and got one of our patrols to come and get a sick German officer who was unable to get out of bed—that when the patrol arrived she urged them to shoot him through the door rather than to take him prisoner?

"That's how your door got perforated. She's an active old girl and a true French patriot. She amazes me. Every night she tells me more, and frankly, General, I'd hate to have that old girl on my tail."

He paused. "These things she tells you are probably her disordered imagination doing her tricks," I hazarded. "She is physically unable to do them."

He shook his head. "No, she is well known here in the city. Several people have told me of her. The evildoers really fear her—and you too—for they think she will tell you what she has already told me."

I pondered it as we went along and then dismissed the matter in favor of more pressing and important things.

As December rolled along and the weather steadily worsened, we began to follow closely the situation on the other front for we were hopefully eager to leave this forgotten one. Then came the Bulge battle and our orders to the Third Army.

Another Division was coming to relieve us. My intention, now, was to build up in the minds of the Germans facing us, the conviction that, having been reinforced, we were preparing to attack them. Every move of relieving units towards the line was by day. Every movement out of the line by night. Other measures were taken. As for the movement of my Headquarters, that was to be most carefully done. I elected to evacuate my own billet at three-thirty in the morning, an hour when all honest townspeople should be sleeping soundly.

I gave the necessary orders to the Chief of Staff and notified the CG of the relieving unit. Secrecy was impressed upon each one. My units began to move from their concentration centers and it was time for me to turn over my Headquarters and go.

Promptly at three-fifteen my escort was at the door. Jeeps were packed with weapons and ammunition and my aides were both busy supervising. It was important that each one be packed in proper order and with the correct amount, for in case of need there would be no time to search.

When I came down the stairs my staff was still filing out one by one, as each was ready. There in the dim hallway near the opened door was *Mademoiselle*. Impervious to the bitter damp predawn waves of frosted chill, which surged through the open door, she stood as rigid and still as a sculptured woman. Her face was transfigured. Every feature was hard set and grim. Her deep eyes moved in satisfaction from one face to another. As each officer with his load squeezed through the narrow door, her hand rested lightly on his shoulder for an instant and a firm deep toned voice which I had difficulty in recognizing as *Mademoiselle's* said "Kill them, my friends. Kill them every one."

I stood motionless on the stairs unwilling to interrupt.

Shades of Jeanne d'Arc, of Charles Martel, of Marshal Foch! I was looking at the bared soul of old France. God grant that the modern one might be as strong! This was the spirit I had known in '17 and had missed now in '45. It had survived. It was alive!

My turn now. I turned toward *Mademoiselle*, moving sidewise to clear my carbine slung over my right shoulder. *Mademoiselle's* hand rested for an instant on my arm—her face came close to mine, her dark eyes; all pupils now, gazed deeply into mine: "*Tuez-les-donc, mon General*," she said firmly, "we have great need..." Her voice trailed off into nothing. Face to face we stood silent. I took her face in both my hands and in respectful French fashion kissed her, first on one cheek and then on the other.

Her bony frame shook with sobs. Both her arms were around my neck, as she wept unrestrainedly for a moment. Then as quickly she recovered. Again, her grave, grim self.

"*Au 'voir Mamselle*," I said and closed the door behind me.

"*Au 'voir, bonne chance!*" came in that haunting high-pitched whisper through the door.

I have never seen Mlle. since. My wife sends her food packages. Still I do feel that the soul of France is not dead. I have seen it—living.

Au 'voir, Mademoiselle.

"Charlie"

It is given to few people to be able to visualize a true cross-section of the youth of our country. To far fewer it is given to see such a cross section assembled in a single unit. Those of us who were members of draft divisions in the last war had this inestimable privilege.

These divisions were made up of representatives from every state, their members, except for the officers, had been selected by the local draft boards, and, in the case of our division, at least, were received directly from the induction centers without passing through the training centers. Consequently, they had nothing to unlearn.

They arrived almost simultaneously in trains from all over the United States. When the work attending their arrival had died down, we began to compile some statistics. They were, indeed, revealing. We found that our average age was twenty-six; we had with us some fourteen sects and religions; practically every trade and profession was represented; and in groups of fifteen or more, we spoke fluently some twenty-eight languages.

Just before we were to take off for the Port of Embarkation en route to the European Theater of Operations, we received an order to the effect that we could not take outside the continental limits of the United States, any man who could not speak and understand English. There may have been some provisions for illiterates, I can not remember, but the order was a rigid one and gave me a certain amount of apprehension. The reason and logic behind the order was obvious, but the job of separating a good soldier from a prideful squad leader, who had trained him for a year or so, to say nothing of the Platoon Commander, had some of the aspects of trying to get a bone away from a hungry dog. Still, orders were orders. The bad news was duly issued and an inspection was scheduled to see that the order was being carried out.

When the inspection party came up on the flank of the leading company of one of my best battalions, I glanced along the front rank. The lads of foreign extraction stood out to me like the black keys on a piano keyboard. By this time, naturally enough, the underground, which works night and day in every good division, would have warned all hands of the purpose of the inspection.

There was a decided amount of self conscientiousness among the men. Squarely in the center of the front rank I spotted a lad of Chinese origin. As we passed slowly along, I talked to the Battalion Commander who had taken his place on my right.

"That Chinese, can he speak and understand English? Have you reported him for transfer out?"

"No, Sir, I haven't reported him. He's all right. He's not very good at it, but he understands all right. He's a fine soldier, Sir, has never failed anything in training. He has never fallen out on the quick fast marches, nor the long ones. He's a favorite with the company and his squad leader. He'll do, Sir, and I'm glad you notice him."

Before I was within six files of him, the victim came up to the "Inspection Arms" ready to get it over. I stopped in front of him. Hard to come by good soldiers. We needed them. A hell of a note to have to get rid of them after such a long and strenuous training. The Battalion Commander had hit me, as he well knew, in a very tender spot. The man's outfit was spotless. His face was expressionless. Taut and rigid as polished amber, he stood there in the torrid Mississippi sun.

"Do you understand what 1 am saying?" I asked. I fear that I would have been satisfied with a nod. His eyes were focused far out beyond the horizon. There was no change in his stance, not a muscle moved. He stood there silent, scarcely breathing and we were at an impasse.

I returned to the charge. "Your name?" I asked "Your organization, what is it? Speak up." He must have been asked these questions hundreds of times. No response, no change in attitude, or expression. This was too much for the sorely tried Battalion Commander. He passed quickly around me to confront our impassive soldier.

"Speak to the General, Charlie," he implored, "for God's sake, say something." I did my best to fight down the contagious wave of mirth sweeping over the younger spirits of the inspection party. The Battalion Commander, now all red in the face, caught the Chinese by the sleeve. "Say something," he roared.

Slowly the eyes of the man came back from that remote spot beyond the horizon. For the first time, he seemed aware that we were there. He hesitated, and then in the most dignified manner addressed us, "*Hensing tao lo mansi mandolot*"—at least it sounded something like that. His voice droned on and the surge of mirth behind me drove me hastily ahead. I did not look back at the party, but resumed my march along the rank.

I could not resist a shot at the Battalion Commander. "You certainly did well with that one, let's see what else you've got." He came along in silence for a while, but the man was on his mind.

"He does understand English. I've talked to him myself many times. He understands it, too." I settled the matter then and there by directing the Personnel Officer to take the man's name and to make certain that he was on the list to be transferred out. The Battalion Commander was crestfallen. That night we received our movement orders to Kilmer and embarkation.

It was in one of our mid-winter attacks on the Siegfried Switch line that I next saw "Charlie." We had penetrated into one of the German's most sensitive areas. A spirited German counter-attack had cut one of our units in two. I spent most of the night with the Regimental Commander in his command post in a very cold and wet cellar in a small German village.

The fighting in the village had been grim and this was the only cellar sound enough to keep out the snow and wind. The Regimental Commander was working hard to determine the amount of the penetration and to re-establish contact with his units on the far side of the gap. His reserves had been committed long since, and every patrol sent out seemed simply to disappear in the darkness.

The radio was silent.

No contact.

Nothing.

It was well along towards midnight, when the blackout curtains were parted and a soldier stumbled in. He stood blinking in the raw light of the Coleman lanterns. His helmet was gone and he was literally caked in ice-cold mud. He absently wiped the blood from a fresh face wound with one muddy hand; in the other, he clutched tightly the yellow first sheet of a field message notebook. The Regimental Sergeant Major seated at his field desk, spotted him. "Come here Charlie, give it to me," he said quietly—very quietly.

There flashed back to me the inspection in Mississippi. The Chinese stepped quickly forward, noted my presence by a rigid attention, and in a firm voice said, "Here me come." He handed the message to the Sergeant Major. The Sergeant Major glanced quickly through it and turned to me and the Regimental Commander.

"It's OK now, Sir, you can go home and get some sleep. Charlie has just come from the company on the other side of the gap. We're all hooked up again and they are rounding up the Germans still in the hole." His eye turned back to the soldier.

"Here, two of you," he gestured to the clerks in the corner, "take Charlie over to the straw, and lay him down. Put a blanket over him. Call the medic. Can't you see he's wounded?" Two men hastened to put an arm each around the sagging man and lead him away.

As he went by me I was startled to hear that same familiar sonorous voice.

"*Umya cheng tao pin tampai*," it said. Charlie was back again in his native tongue. I have always wondered what he said. It must have been good. At any rate, my conscience is clear. The Battalion Commander was right and I was wrong. He could speak English. I heard him.

The White Bird

The hero of this story, Nungesser, was a French peasant who, although only semi-literate, rose to national adulation during WWI and a few years beyond. He was well known to my father who as a young officer was assigned to the U.S. Army Ordinance Branch with a mission to assist the French Air Force in developing weaponry for fighter and bomber aircraft between 1916–1918. Nungesser was a barracks mate and, according to my father's description, was as cold blooded as they come. His most prominent physical feature was his eyes, which were absolutely dead, with no expression at all. Prior to flying a mission he would usually be lying on his cot in the barracks staring at the ceiling oblivious to all around him.

Nungesser was the number one Ace of Allied fighter pilots and was said to be the equal of Baron Von Richthofen, the German Ace. The story, which follows, traces his history until his surprising end.

The White Bird

Nungesser's daydream was interrupted by the clanging of the church bell in his little rural village on the border between France and Belgium. Normally the church bell was rung only on Sundays or religious holidays; at any other time it signified an emergency of some magnitude. Nungesser unhitched his plow horse from the plow he was using in preparing his fields for planting; placed his military saddle, was issued by the government to him and to all members of the militia, on its back and raced off to the village square. There he was informed that as it appeared German patrols were probing into France the militia in the village were directed to reconnoiter. The young men, flush with excitement, raced off to their homes to grab their militia issued rifles, bayonets, homespun uniforms and galloped off pell mell to deal with the German patrols.

As the militia galloped across the fields where the patrols were reported, they were cut down like so many sheaves of wheat by machine gun fire. All were killed almost immediately, except Nungesser whose dead horse had fallen on him thus saving his life.

Little did he realize that his group had run head on to the point of the main German Army which was sweeping through Belgium in the now historical military maneuver called *Kid und Kessel* (Arm and Hammer). The "Hammer," the main striking force, was steam rolling everything in its path, and was well on its way to Paris at the time.

Nungesser, though dazed, was unhurt and with some difficulty extricated himself from under the horse, grabbed his rifle and set out in the direction of his village to give warning. As he entered a wooded area, he heard German voices and following the sounds he came upon a clearing in which 4 or 5 German officers were huddled around a large map, spread on the hood of their staff car.

Recognizing them as the hated *Boche*, he shot all of them, grabbed the map, stole the car[2], and headed towards a nearby main road. Unfortunately, the road was full of German Infantry soldiers on both sides on their way to Paris. Nungesser, at full throttle, drove down the middle of the road and was almost through the column when the Germans realized that a French militiaman should not be driving a German staff car and showered him with rifle shots.

Nungesser drove the shot up car into Paris and clanged into the city on its tire rims with the captured map clutched tightly. The *gendarmes*, upon being asked for directions to Field Marshall Foch's headquarters thought he was drunk or crazy when he kept telling them that the Germans were attacking. Finally after much shouting and waving of arms, he made his way to the headquarters. There ensued more shouting and cursing as Nungesser demanded to see the Field Marshall himself. Hearing all of the racket, Foch came out to see the cause of the disturbance and there was the disheveled, bruised, militiaman driving a German staff car with bullet holes claiming that the German Army was invading France. Improbably, the militiaman was waving some sort of map in the air.

Nungesser whose only mission, in his own eyes, was to deliver the map to the proper authorities, pressed the map on Foch who opened it and recoiled in surprise AS IT WAS THE ORDER OF BATTLE FOR TOTAL ARM AND HAMMER MANEUVER!

The next day Foch called Nungesser to his office and in gratitude offered him a field commission in the French Cavalry as a reward. Nungesser indicated that he had had enough of Cavalry type war and that he had more than served his time in that particular branch. Foch

---

[2]The French Ministry of Agriculture, encouraging the use of modern farm equipment, had a program of teaching farmers to operate tractors thus driving the stolen car war practical.

then asked him what branch of the service he desired and was informed by Nungesser that he wanted to be a flier. Foch then wrote a note for him to carry to Orly Airfield the next day.

With that note, France's premier air ace was created. My father was stationed at Orly in 1917 which was the training center for French fliers and was the Barracks mate of Nungesser whom he described as a man consumed by killing—he was described as a man with eyes as hard as steel ball bearings, who in preparing for missions would, as previously noted, be perfectly still staring at the ceiling until it was time to go.

I'm not sure how many kills were registered to Nungesser but as a guess, I would say 60 to 80. [3]

Nungesser was a national hero and was idolized by the French during and after the war.

In about 1920 Nungesser and his wartime navigator undertook to cross the Atlantic to America—a national subscription was undertaken to build an aircraft especially designed to make the almost suicidal flight. The French aeronautical engineers proudly presented an aircraft with huge single wings spanning far in excess of any aircraft at that time, it was painted all white and was widely proclaimed as *The White Bird*. In 1927 the *White Bird* with Nungesser and his navigator flew off into the mists of the Atlantic never to be seen again. The nation was saddened, but in time it came to terms that the *Bird* had fallen into the ocean and Nungesser had perished.

In 1943, a Canadian postal plane was flying over a particularly barren part of Labrador and spied an object, which had crashed in the wilderness. Closer inspection showed that it was the *Bird*. Nungesser had made it! Thus becoming the first flier to cross the Atlantic and he did it the long way! The causes of the crash have never been made public.

---

[3] Nungesser ended WWI with 43 recorded victories

The *Apache*

> Navarre was second to Nungesser for kills in WWI and in temperament was the direct opposite of him. Navarre was also known to my father, as judging from his account, he not only was a gangster, but also a "wild man"! Apparently, he was also fearless, and never saw a drink he didn't like. This account shows just how wild Navarre really was, unfortunately he was killed while practicing to fly through the Arc de Triomphe and France lost its most colorful ace.

The *Apache*

Apache (pronounced in France as AN-POSH) is the term used to describe denizens of the underworld in and around the Port of Marseilles in southern France. There is also a type of dance known as *Apache*, which originated in Marseilles. There is no relationship to a once feared American Indian tribe called Apache (AH-PATCH-EE) by others, except the element of raucousness.

Navarre was born on 8 August 1895 in Jouy-sur-Morin and was *Apache* of the lowest order; he was in trouble with the French *gendarmes* in almost every major city in France and was rumored to have killed more than one man in fights involving knives, pistols, etc. Obviously he was a man around whom one walked carefully.

As this story starts, Navarre was in a Paris jail awaiting trial for killing a *gendarme* who tried to arrest him for some offense or another, undoubtedly while he was drunk.

Well, there is one thing I forgot to mention—Navarre was, next to Nungesser, the Ace fighter pilot in the French Air Force in WWI. His record of kills of German pilots was almost equal to Nungesser at that time. By reputation he was absolutely fearless and flew like a madman who celebrated wildly after each kill.

The German Army had advanced to within 90 miles of Paris and was lobbing shells from "Big Bertha" their long distance cannon into the suburbs of Paris. As the shelling increased the Parisians started to panic and were calling for miracles to halt the German advance. Part of this call for miracles was to free Navarre—Navarre and Nungesser will save them from the dreaded *Boche*. As the pressure grew, the authorities decided to parole Navarre on the condition that he would immediately report to Orly Airfield and be ready to "defend France."

As a morale booster, the authorities scheduled a flying exhibition at Orly by Navarre to show all of France that indeed Navarre was now free and that France would be saved. Navarre was released on a Saturday and the exhibition was scheduled for Sunday.

On schedule with a sizable crowd cramming the bleachers erected for the occasion, Navarre stumbled bleary eyed from his Saturday night celebration of his freedom and climbed into his plane.

Instead of sedately taxiing down the tarmac, he set his brakes and gunned his engine to the maximum speed. As the brakes started to tremble with the strain, he suddenly released them and the plane was launched like a rocket almost straight up. Once up to about 5000 feet he performed all of the standard aerial tactics; the Immelman, the Inside Loop, etc.

As the crowd was "oohing" and "aahing," Navarre climbed to 10,000 feet which was about the maximum in those days and before the horrified gaze of the crowd attempted an Outside Loop—a maneuver which had never been successfully completed before as the wings of the plane could not stand the strain and would be ripped off.

Navarre, however, seemed to feel that ordinary physics of flight didn't apply to him. His attempt was halted by his crashing into the tarmac from several thousand feet. The plane itself was a mass of cloth, wires, parts of the engine, and God knows what else—the crowd was in shock as the ambulance and fire engines sped out to locate the victim and to keep the wreckage from exploding because of the volatility of the gasoline.

As the ambulance drove up they could see an arm and a leg in the pile of materials which had once been the plane; slowly the arm and leg moved and Navarre struggled to extricate himself from the pile. As he staggered to his feet before the incredulous spectators, he started to grope around his chest and stomach.

"Oh!" cried the crowd, "Navarre is injured: maybe he is dying." As the medics from the ambulance approached him, they suddenly saw him extract a packet of cigarettes from his jacket which was soaked with gasoline and put a similarly soaked cigarette into his mouth. He further had in his hand a kitchen match which be was trying to strike to light the cigarette; the danger from this was far greater than diving into the earth from 10,000

feet. He was led away and found to be 100% physically fit.
  He died in 1919.

The Guard Post

In the early days of the modern Field Artillery, the Old Post of San Antonio was commanded by a fine old soldier of vast experience and understanding who we shall call Graybill. His rank of Colonel had been gained for many years on the Plains and his sense of duty was of the old standard.

Once in a while, in order to check the performance of guard duty Captains and Lieutenants of his command, he would make an after midnight inspection of the guard. This was very great trial to all the Garrison for when Old Man was hurried about anything he invariably stuttered to such a degree that a startled sentry or an officer of the Guard was quite unable to pull himself together enough to recite his orders. These the Old Man always asked.

One night when we were having a blinding rain, the Colonel elected to make one of his after midnight rounds. He started with the Number One sentry who, in those days was always stationed at the Guard House. This sentry was wrapped round in a poncho and had his rifle well slung under it. His hat was pulled over his eyes and he heard nothing of the approach of the Colonel.

His first notice of the rounds came as he rounded the corner of the guardhouse and crashed into the Old Man. This was no ordinary crash, but a full souled one. The sentry recovered first, unslung his rifle and did as good a "Present Arms" as he could.

The Old Man recovered his balance and turned to his Inspection. "Y-Y-Y-You," he sputtered, "don't you ever look where y-y-y-you're going?"

The sentry stood very patiently "Y-Y-Yes S-s-s-sir, I g-g-g-generally do."

"W-W-W-What in the h-h-hell", said the Old Man, "are you trying to do M-m-m-mimic me?"

"N-N-No Sir," said the sentry, "I-I-stutter, too."

"You do?" said the Old Man, "W-W-What damned fool enlisted you?"

"Y-Y-You did S-s-sir," said the sentry.

The Colonel returned the sentry's salute and disappeared in the darkness.

Then there was the sentry who was stationed at the Number One Post during the visit of a Foreign Minister. The Officer of the Day had carefully instructed him as to his duties and had borne down hard on the call to "Turn out the Guard." He had the sentry repeat several times the proper call: "Turn out the Guard, Chinese Minister."

The Minister had to pass the Guard House on his way from the train. The Guard was polished up waiting for the call when the carriage arrived just opposite the Guard House. Number One faced the carriage with great precision, came down to a "Port Arms" and called in a tone audible all over the area:

"Turn out the Guard," he roared, "Chinese Preacher."

The Sentry told the Summary Court Officer later that any way the Guard damn well turned out.

Uncivil War

Pinky Sard returned from the polo tournament in Manila to find his happy home in a complete turmoil. In the Southern Islands where the single cavalry squadron eked out a quiet existence with the Moros, Pinky's house was noted for the quietly ordered hospitality it dispensed and Pinky was more than displeased.

He was a quiet, efficient redheaded Major whose blue eyes could snap when the occasion demanded. They were snapping now.

As befitted a bachelor of some standing, he was served by two Filipino boys whose every effort had appeared to be spent in anticipating his desires. Now, where there had been harmony there was hostility. Felipe, the cook, appeared with a black eye; Juan, the houseboy, had a pair of badly skinned knuckles. The evidence was there for all to see.

After interviewing them both together, Pinky had dismissed Juan and was working on Felipe. "Tell me about it, now, Felipe. Talk fast and it had better be good," he barked. "What was this fight about and who started it?"

Felipe shifted from one foot to the other. "You no sooner gone," he said, "then that darn Juan he come in here. He sit down in the Major's chair. He help himself to the Major's cigarettes. He go to the icebox and take out whiskey. He make himself highball and he lean back in chair and put his feet on table. This more than I can stand. I say to him, 'Who do you think you are—god-damned Army Officer?' He jump up and then we fight."

Pinky shook his head sadly and dismissed the boy. He had to think this one over.

Erin Go Braugh!

The other day I received a letter from my son-in-law, who served with the British and French troops before our own Army was fully organized as a separate entity, and who tells the following story.

When the 88th Division was in training, they had as an Inspector on duty with the Division One Captain Finnegan, of the British Army. The captain was a very mild mannered man, but he had numerous decorations, and had been quite seriously wounded from which he was recovering at the time. But no one thought of him in the lights of a fire eater as his manner was so mild, and they were quite surprised when they arrived in England to hear on of Finnegan's brother officers tell the following story on him.

One cold night up in the trenches, Finnegan received a parcel from home. He opened it with care; it was his delight to find two quarts of Scotch Whiskey. He and another Lieutenant, for he was only a subaltern then, went into his dugout and drank it all up. In the wee small hours Finnegan waxed belligerent; he was aching for a fight. He could not be dissuaded; outside he went and aroused his platoon. He told them he was tired of this sitting around; he wanted a fight, a real fight; and he wanted some men to follow him and they would go over and give the *Boches* a taste of cold steel.

Being an Irish Brigade, you can guess the result; every man volunteered.

Finnegan picked out fifteen, and over they went. Soon they reached the *Boche* wire and were discovered. The *Boche* called for reinforcements, and a company was rushed to the scene.

The other Lieutenant, seeing the scrap waxed hot, brought over the rest of the platoon. By this time the Captain had been informed, and as the German company began to get in its work, he asked his Battalion Commander to go over with the rest of the Company. Soon the Major thought he had better take over the Battalion for the *Boches* were still coming; the Brigade Commander became interested, and soon another

Battalion was sent over. Quite soon the whole division was engaged along a front of ten kilometers, in a pretty little scrap of their own that all grew out of Finnegan's fighting jag. Where, except in an Irish division, could such things happen?

Mounted Murder

The three of us sat there quietly enjoying the Texas morning. An old Dodge roadster sped along the road throwing a following thin cloud of dust and its occupants waved cheerily at us.

We were buying horses and the owners of the Bar-Three Ranch were happy to see us for the country was still in the very throes of the famous depression and they had not sold a horse for nearly a year.

Captain Jerry Aguas and I were the ones upon whom the Bar-Three hoped would prove their benefactors to the point where they could pay off some of their creditors. Glen Crofield, one of the Bar-Three partners, sat on the running board of the battered old car which our generous government had furnished us while he waited for the other partner to arrive. We were to look at his herd of young animals; he knew, on behalf of the government, we would pay cash.

"That was Pappy Fleet in that car," said Jerry and caught Glen's eye. They both smiled and I realized that I was standing on the outside of something amusing.

"What did Pappy do to you, Glen?" Pappy was in charge of the Reno Remount Station and an authority on horses.

"He didn't do anything. I did it all, myself. But I think Pappy was responsible. Anyway, if hadn't been for him, nothin' would have happened."

"Well, go ahead. What happened?"

"I might as well tell you. If I don't you'll get it all out of Jerry.

"You know that this past year has been the worst in our lives. We hadn't sold many horses and it looked as though we weren't goin' to do much better now. Well, I got an idea that if we could train some of these ponies of our'n to play polo, we might pick up a sale or two to some of these lads from the big teams who were on the lookout for ponies and who had got the cash to pay for 'em. So Paul and I and a coupla' the other lads borrowed some wore-out balls from Pappy and he gave us each a polo stick to help us along.

"I don't think that any of us had ever seen a polo game, although there

95

had been games all around us, but we went to work on the ponies slow and easy and we trained them over there in that corral which we hadn't been using for a long time."

Glen took off his hat and dusted it against his leg and his gray blue eyes took on a quizzical squint, the prelude to a tale.

"They were getting along good—not tryin' to duck the stick and showing right good spirit in pushin' each other off the ball.

"Well, Pappy came along a coupla days later and we was playin' over there in the corral a-hittin' the ball as best we could. From where I was seated, I could see the floor of the corral as shiny and as slippery as a well-waxed dance floor and I could picture four horses with four reckless riders aboard galloping full tilt in that restricted space."

"Mounted murder," I muttered.

"Maybe, but it was fun an' that was all we were. Getting out of our herd, anyway.

"Well, we didn't see Pappy, but he saw us all right and the next thing we know there he is standin' behind the corral fence a-yellin' at us to come over there.

"'You're goin' great,' he shouts. 'That's what'll do it. You bring them horses up where they kin be seen,' he says, 'an' you'll sell 'em. If I had any money myself I'd buy 'em. More'n that,' he says, 'you're developin' a fine team of polo players too. An' that's what interests me right now. A Cowboy Polo Team! That'll pack 'em in. That's exactly what I need. Now, we're havin' a little polo tournament up to Reno next month. It starts on the sixteenth. You boys come up there and bring your ponies. I kin almost guarantee you'll sell some horses.'

"Paul started to say somethin', but you know Pappy. He didn't give him a chance. 'We don't know nothin' about polo,' I says. 'We never even seen a game.'

"'I'll leave you a book that tells all about it,' he yells and hurries to his car and comes back with an official rulebook. 'If you think you can't understand it, get one of them Bailey brothers down the road to help you,' he says. 'I'm almost sure that the oldest one played some. I'm in a hurry, or I'd stay and go through it with you.' With that he gets in his car and drives off as fast as he can make it go.

"Pedro Vaca and John Diaz, who were ridin' with me and Paul, now rode up and said that Pappy was crazy as a loon and that they were married and had lots of relatives in this part of Texas and they were not going to Reno nor any other place to play Polo.

"They felt that it was not a game, but more risky than robbin' the mails and they wanted no part of it. If they won, they had made nothin'; if they lost the chances were that the relatives who had the poor judgment to bet on their team would regard the outcome as a personal affront and we knew what that meant.

"Well, I remembered what Pappy had said about the Bailey brothers, and I wasn't too sorry to see the boys backing out and anyway someone had to stay back to take care of the ranch and maybe to bury the dead.

"We talked it over that night and agreed that we were in business to sell horses; that we hadn't had much luck at it while things were down like they were. It looked as though maybe, if Pappy were right, we might sell some. It would cost us only the oil and gas for the truck to get there and we finally decided to go.

"The Bailey boys were keen for the game. They said that Pappy was our friend; that we had ponies and why not make a try at sellin' some. They had played, but never a real game and they wanted to try it. It was a line game and we would certainly do better than we thought we could.

"So we borrowed some more stuff from Jerry, there, and kept on training the ponies. Paul and I consoled each other by sayin' that it was only a little tournament—Pappy had said so—and even if we did as badly as we prob'ly would, none of our friends need to be told.

"So, finally came the day. We tried not to say much to each other for we didn't feel too good about our chances. We loaded the horses in the truck and then the five of us got in as best we could and we were off for Reno. There were five of us for Pedro Vaca and John Diaz had both shown up, havin' changed their minds and now were eager to go. We took Pedro, but John had to stay behind to take care of the herd.

"The ride up was fine. It was a beautiful day an' we didn' hit much traffic until we were through Oklahoma City, but from there on to Reno, the roads were crowded. Paul kept looking at all this crowd a-goin' the same way and asks me where in hell I thought they were all bound. I didn't know. I told him to ask 'em. So when we all stopped for a red light, he leaned out and asks the nearest fella' and this fella told him that he was goin' to Reno to see the polo games. The man was all dressed up and had a nice lookin' gal with him. She kept lookin' at the horses in our truck and says to the man that we was kiddin' him for we were taking ponies to the game.

"Paul was right upset about it. 'Just like I said,' he yammered, 'we'll be the laughin' stock of the hull damned southwest. We gotta get outta this mess someway.'

"Well, I sorta agreed with him, but the Bailey boys said that that wasn't the way to look at it at all. We come up here to sell polo ponies and to do that we had to play a little polo so the purchasers could see what the horses could do. They weren't interested in what we could do for they hadn't any intention of buying us to play polo. It was the horses.

"That seemed right enough, too. But Paul kept growlin' and finally I cheered him up a little by tellin' him that we could watch a game or two before we played—Pappy had said there were a lot of other teams entered—and pick up some tricks of the game. After all, there wasn't much to it. Just a lot of hard ridin' which we did every day and a-hittin' a ball. That oughtn't be too much.

"When we got into Reno, we found Pappy quite busy. He was doin' about everything they was to be done. He just took enough time out to hand me a fifth of good whiskey, point out a pyramidal tent where we were to live, and tell me that he would be up to see us as soon as we got settled and had tied up our horses on the picket line.

"Pappy was as good as his word. He found us all sittin' on the bunks tryin' to figure how we could get away. Still, we wanted to sell horses and we couldn't do both. Pappy wouldn't hear of our goin'. 'Nothin' to it. You can ride rings around any team here. Just wait till I get back. I gotta go and be present for the team drawin'. That's to pair off the teams to play each other.' He gulped down his drink and left at a lope.

"Maybe it was Pappy's confidence and maybe it was the whiskey, but the fact is that we felt better for Pappy's visit. Pedro Vaca said the horses came through in good shape and everything simmered down to wait for Pappy's return.

"He come back about noon and told us where to go for chow and then took our appetites away by tellin' us, 'You're lucky again,' he said. 'You've drawn the first game and you're goin' to play Annydarko.' He hit Paul on the back. 'An' I just put up five dollars on you boys to win.'

"Paul was mad all the way through. 'You know, Pappy that we don't know a damn thing about this game, don't you? None of us, except maybe the Bailey boys, have ever played and outside these two we ain't never even seen a game. We'll be the laughin' stock of the Southwest. The only thing favorin' us so far is that I ain't seen any of my friends here to laugh at us...' But Pappy broke in.

"'I'm goin' to tell you how to beat this Annydarko bunch, for you can do it. Now, listen to me. You can beat 'em by ridin'. You can ride better than any of them. Now, you just ride. That's your main thing. Ride 'em off. Don't let any of 'em get a free shot at the ball. Keep ridin' them way you were doin' it down in that corral of your'n. Of course, you gotta hit the ball when you can—an' hit it the right way, towards your own goal. But you concentrate on ridin' them. You'll win. Eat light and be ready to saddle up at one-thirty.'

"We ate light all right. I guess only the Bailey boys and Pedro took anything at all. We were ready to go at one thirty when Pappy came dashin' up to the picket line and told us how to line up for throwin' in the ball.

"Somebody blew a horn and Pappy yelled, 'Remember what I told you. Ride 'em and you're in.'

"Well, we lined up with the help of the referee. Someone tossed a nice white ball down and one of the Bailey boys hit it and then the damndest scurryin' around took place, I ever seen. Men ridin' horses in every direction at once. I just set there. Then I remembered what Pappy had said and looked around for some of the fellers from Annydarko. I picked out one on a fine lookin' big bay with a white star, snip and blaze on 'im and, brother, I rode him. It was getting to be fun.

"He tried to duck me in every way he could, but I saw to it that he never got near the ball. He took off down the field and I lost him for a minute and then somebody rung a bell. Everything stopped all of a sudden.

"What's that?" I asked the younger Bailey. "What's that mean?" He looked at me a second and allowed that Annydarko had just got a goal.

"Before I could ask any more questions, they lined us up again and throwed in another ball and off again we went. This time I got goin' better and even had a coupla chances at the ball. The first time I hit the ground about six inches behind it. But the second shot, I really socked it. It rose off the ground and went over the withers of one of the Annydarko horses and the feller ridin' ducked way down. Then I remembered that I was to find an Annydarko player and ride him.

"I found him all right, a-streakin' down the field way over by the side boards and I kept between him and the play. He never had a chance.

"All of a sudden there was another gong sounded. 'Now what,' I asked the younger Bailey. He looked plumb put out. 'Annydarko, agin.' He says, 'They got another goal.'

"Well, almost right away they blowed that horn agin' and we rode in to change horses. It was the end of the chuller, they said.

"Pappy was there waitin'. He stormed and swore. 'Whut did I tell you?'

he yelled at me. 'What did I say the last thing. Did I er didn't I tell you to ride your opponents? You, Glen Crofield,' he screamed. 'You're the one done it all. It was your man, you were supposed to be ridin' thet shot both them goals. He oughta shot about a thousand, the way you didn't get near him. You're the feller responsible fer them goals.'

"This was more than I had to take. 'You're wrong, Pappy,' I roared back at him. 'Damn good an' wrong. I rode my man just like you told me. He didn't git anywhere near the ball. He didn't shoot no goals. He was lucky I let him stay on the field.'

"I looked around an' here came a-ridin' thet big bay with the star snip, and blaze. 'Look, Pappy here he comes, now. See. He's got so mad he throwed his stick away.' Pappy give one look and liked to choke. 'Thet, Glen,' he says, 'Thet, Glen's the referee.'"

When I had recovered enough to speak audibly, "Glen," I asked, "did you sell any horses?"

"Yeah. One. The one I was ridin'. The referee bought him."

The Refined One

> I have always appreciated rural humor, it's always rough and usually picturesque, but, most of all, it's direct and to the point and reflects the environment around the raconteur. Anyone who was brought up in the Dust Bowl of Oklahoma fully appreciates the character of the "Okies" who in spite of the poverty, hunger, and hardship around them in the 1930's maintained their sense of humor and personal dignity. This story by my father reflects the spirit of these people.

The Refined One

One of my friends who was afflicted with a hare lip, and who in addition stuttered, used to start his tales, all worthy of great mirth, by saying, "When I was young and used to smoke and drink and run around with the women..."

I am writing this tale in much the same spirit for it occurred so many years ago, that I am afraid to recall it.

At that time, I was stationed in Oklahoma. I liked the Oklahomans for a number of reasons. They were of the old American I'll take-a-chance-if-you-will type and while they were right sudden, generally they were kindly, modest people. Like them the climate was chancy and after the prairie got broken up, particularly in the Panhandle, the long droughts and the dust storms which accompanied them, burned up all the grass to the great loss of the entire cattle industry.

There had been no rain for many months and something had to be done to save what remained of the herds, which were dying on the hoof.

The cattlemen got together and decided that the only thing left for them to do was to organize a drive and move their herds up to Colorado where the grass was green and plentiful. There was no difficulty in getting permission to graze their herds on the public lands there.

A movement such as that planned required the same kind of a reconnaissance that had to be made to move an Infantry Division and I told everyone I knew that I would very much like to go along. You can well imagine the many details to be settled: the roads to be crossed by thousands of cattle to the great impediment of travel; arrangements for watering and feeding or grazing; the cutting of fences—all the little detailed things which if forgotten could cause all kinds of trouble to both ranchers and animals alike.

I was lucky enough to be offered an invitation, and accepted with alacrity. My Commanding Officer was glad to have me go as a public relations gesture.

The heat and dust were still terrific when we started out to make the arrangements. I think that it was about the second day of our auto travel that we arrived at a little crossroads town named Chapsall. The sun was getting a bit down, but that is the hottest part of the day. There was no wind and, I noticed that as we came into the town, there were several large herds of cattle gathered in the shade of the hills, where the shadows were starting to turn a little purple.

When I presumed to ask Old Man Robertson (who was the top man in this show) how come all these cattle were there with only a couple of cow hands riding herd, he laughed with that rusty hinge laugh of his and said, "I'll show you, Major. An' more than that, I'm surprised you ask. Don't tell me that you don't know Essie." I said, "No, I don't," and he went on.

"We might as well eat here, for we've plenty of miles to go yet. I'll introduce you to Essie. She's the only gal in this county and the reason them steers is there is because all the boys are over to Essie's diner talkin' to her."

We rounded the bend in the road and there before my astounded eyes was a regular trolley car diner squatting there on the empty prairie.

Our arrival caused no comment. We mounted the empty stools and Old Man Robertson, after returning the greetings of all the cowhands, preserved the protocol by introducing me to Essie.

"Essie, this here is a friend of mine, Major Malony."

"Pleased to meet you," said Essie.

"Please to meet you, too," said I.

The amenities finished, Old Man Robertson started a real bombardment.

"Essie, I heard a few things the other day which I want to check up on."

"Yes, Mr. Robertson." Essie seemed to take his belligerent approach with great calmness. She turned to look in the mirror behind the cash register and tucked a stray lock of her black hair out of the way.

"Is it true, Essie, that you're about to make the greatest mistake in your life by marryin' that long geared, lantern jawed, cow hand who lives up around Crittenden—that Lon Simmons?"

"It sure is, Mr. Robertson." No hesitation and no blush. All the cowhands on their stools, with broad grins was watching this pretty scene.

"Well, Essie, how come you picked that gawky fella over all these fine lookin' boys settin' here? Now how come? D'you mind tellin' me that?"

"Like I said, Mr. Robertson, Lon and I are engaged to be married. You know, he used to come here every night. I picked him out because"—she put one strong hand on her plump hip—"he seemed so refined."

"Refined, eh? Refined!" Old Man Robertson gazed disbelievingly at the ceiling as tho' calling upon heaven to be his witness. "He's a-getting' you under false pretenses, Essie. That's what he's doin'. Did'ya ever see that guy up at Pendleton for the rodeo, or over to Cheyenne? Essie, he's about the roughest thing in these parts, I cain't understand how a smart gal like you could think that fella was refined. Did he tell you that himself?"

"No. He didn't, Mr. Robertson. I found it out for myself. You know, that when it gets cool and the boys come in here to get their supper, they most generally orders soup. Well, I noticed that all these boys here they blowed them, but Lon fanned his'n with his hat."

Old Man Robertson led the boom of laughter and we unanimously pronounced Essie the winner.

The Half Crown Story

I love this story—it's typically British and to me uproarious!

Picture, if you can, the very proper civil servant of substantial stature being confronted in the manner described.

The irony is just delicious.

The Half Crown Story

Wartime London was no joke. To be there shortly after the Battle for Britain, after Goering the Fat had sold his bill of goods to Hitler, and thought that Britain could be brought to her knees by bombing alone, was to spend one's nights in a man made hell.

The suffering and uncomplaining people made one proud to have come from their stock. Each night was like the preceding one and the moonlight nights were the worst for the city dwellers.

Britain was at a decided disadvantage in the bombings, for while it was a short enough hop from the German held areas to London, the retaliatory hop to Berlin, or to some other profitable city target, was so much longer that, during the short nights, it could not be made without exposure to daylight attack on the return journey.

So, all of London accepted the situation and since sleep was a hard to get commodity, we all quit work, whenever that was possible, to walk ourselves into some sort of exhaustion so that the inevitable night raid might not wake us. Therefore all of London and I mean all, walked when they could from say, five o'clock until seven.

You all know that when an Englishman walks for exercise, he really does a job of it. With arms swinging and chin up, he covers ground like a boxer at his road work—and he hates to be interrupted.

The women were not equally energetic, but occasionally they appeared with that ineradicable air of determination and swing along in the same manner. In those days there was no stop for conversation. Each one generated his own enthusiasm, but then all London walked and the many different types made their way each to their favorite haunts.

In passing, I may say that London had never impressed me as a beautiful city, but during the blackouts and in the period of moonlit nights, it seemed to turn back the clock for itself to those times in the Middle Ages when gentlemen carried their swords with them in their night ventures and expected to use them. The city was always beautiful in the moonlight alone.

The Crown Solicitor of those days was a gallant gentleman who, inclined to suffer somewhat from insomnia, did his best in the late afternoon to develop enough tiredness to last him through the bombing raid that night.

It was on one of these swift and determined efforts, that he came at full speed down Bond Street and made his way through the other walkers, towards Clarges St.

As he arrived at the entrance there, a full blown brunette, dressed in somewhat outdated but glorious attire, stepped into his path and smiled. "'Ullo," she said. He stopped cold, completely astonished.

"'Ullo," she repeated.

I feel sure that never in his official life had the Crown Solicitor met such a situation. He gulped, but quickly recovered. "My dear, you caw'nt do that, you know."

Then in desperation, added, "I am the Crown Solicitor."

She looked the embarrassed man straight in the eye, smiled again and said fetchingly, "Well, fancy that, Guvernor, I'm the half Crown Solicitor."

She turned and smiled brightly over her shoulder and disappeared in the crowd.

One World

I can vouch for this story told by my father. We had a 300 acre farm near a small New Hampshire town name Canaan Street. Yes, that's really the name of the town, and its population might be 1000 (probably less) and it's a suburb of Canaan (population 3000).

Jim Kilton was a handy man who had his own farm, but would help out at our farm when needed.

The inhabitants of Vermont, and New Hampshire had a very dry sense of humor and told stories with their unique New England accents. These people were very hard working: loyal to their friends; thrifty; and extremely shrewd. As in many isolated rural communities throughout the East, there was some inter-mingling with the usual results when carried to the extreme.

One World

If Mr. Wendell Willkie had lived in our neck of the woods in New Hampshire, he would doubtless have gotten some new angles on his One World Theory, for, while we all know that there are other parts of the United States, and we read all about the dirty doings in Laos and Viet Nam for example, it is with our own daily businesses we occupy ourselves and it is with the family which lives a few hundred yards up the road we are concerned.

When a man takes an ax and a maul and some splitting wedges and starts out to spend a day splitting birch in a world which the early fall has painted into a riot of yellows, browns and reds, he suddenly finds that he is alone in spirit, as well as in occupation. Here, if someone comes along, conversation assumes a glory long since gone from this hectically overpopulated land of ours, and one does not just drop it in the dead leaves; rather, he holds it up and turns it this way and that to enjoy all its varied nuances, and to examine each facet in turn.

Last fall, when I was getting my mail from the mailbox in front of the house, down the hill came Jim Kilton who works for me—when he feels the urge—and opposite me, halted his tractor. Jim was wearing a sweater against the cold of the early morning, and one of his cotton hats which many years ago had the name "Eggleston's Store" on its front in bold black letters. He looked across at me and in a deceptively mild way said softly, "Harry," he snapped off his ignition, "I can't think that these funny religious sects we have here in New Hampshire are doin' us not a damn bit o' good."

Now there was an opening gambit not to be lightly disregarded.

I straightened out my face and equally offhandedly allowed that I would like to hear more before I committed myself. Jim went blithely on. "I remember well," he said, "'when that sect now down below Concord come to Dorchester." He paused to see if I were interested.

"What happened?" I had to satisfy the protocol.

"Well, there was a feller headin' that sect who was a real determined sort of a man. He kept goin' round to all the poor chaps livin' there makin' a hell of a nuisance of himself askin' each one to join.

"As a matter of fact, he made such a nuisance of himself that they eventually drove him out o' town. But one mawnin' he come to John Quinby and he says 'John, you gotta join this group. It's one of the best of the modern religions.' I told you he was a determined feller, but old John was even more determined. He looked the feller straight in the eye and said, 'B'God, I wunt.'

"An' for a time that ended that.

"But the feller didn't give up. He got a lot of the women who wanted a little excitement to help out and went around makin' speeches and gettin' joiners, until he finally tackled Ol' John again.

"'John,' he says, 'I've come all the way out here to see you fer this is important. I want to tell you that you just got time to join, now; fer the world, John, the world is a-goin' to end next Thursday.'

"John looked him over coolly enough, 'All right,' sez John. 'Let 'er go. Me. I don't give a damn. I'm goin' over to Vermont on Tuesday.'"

You Can Never Hurt A Drunk: A Villager's Story

Then there was the strange case of the readjustment to scientific progress of Ashabel Hollister Benton. Ashabel held for many years the dubious position of town drunk. He apparently had no competitors worthy of mention. Comparatively speaking, they were hardly in the "also ran" class.

Ashabel was a man of no fixed orbit. His path was truly parabolic, the governing focus being Swoort's Saloon and the Oosterhaut House where he dispensed his labor at general cleaning and odd jobs with careful and studied precision; and balanced his accounts with his alcoholic intake. He was a sturdy sire, the father of four, who were the envy of their contemporaries and the horror of the benign ladies of the town.

The first automobile in the town was the property of one Dr. Ovenshine, the local dentist. Tall and spare with a black mustachio, he was the living embodiment of the devil in the eyes of the small fry whose dental needs he met. Still, he was esteemed a fine citizen of great civic value, and held in high repute as an adventurous and impetuous character. When Doc showed up with his auto—it was a Selden I think—the town was thoroughly alerted to his every mood. It was impossible for him to step quietly on the starter, back out into his driveway, and be off to destination unknown. In the first place, there was no starter. The thing was not simple at all.

The drill went about like this. Doc first put on his linen duster. That was the accepted and conventional mark of the motorist. He next donned a woolen cap with visor worn to the rear. Over his ears he forced a pair of goggles, which finally dangled, loosely from his neck. He took a firm stance beside the car and made sure—very sure—that the clutch was disengaged, and then with almost micrometer precision he set the lever reading "5" for spark on the segment underneath the steering wheel and the one reading "0" for Gas. He withdrew to a position of observation and carefully checked his handiwork.

Then from under the back seat, and the jumble of junk which he carried inside, he brought out the crank. This he handled with all the respect due a lethal weapon. A kickback might mean a broken wrist at least, and Doc's attitude was apprehensive. Grim determination marked his every move for he was about to begin the supreme effort. After considerable groping the crank became engaged and Doc braced himself against the radiator. A few tentative heaves and o-o-over she went.

The first result was an explosion, accompanied by an outburst of a cloud of smoke from the exhaust. Doc could be seen working frantically to withdraw the crank, rush from the front to the side of the car and thrash wildly at the levers labeled "G" and "S".

Almost invariably, after a few tentative explosions, she died. Doc would start the process over again, trying not to hurry. From this point on, he was not alone for the first explosion was enough to bring every urchin in the neighborhood running to the excitement. From this point on, Doc had plenty of volunteers in his enterprise.

He also had many suggestions some of which *sotto voce* bordered on the obscene and vulgar, but he persevered until finally shuddering in every bolt she seemed to have made up her mind to continue running.

Now came Doc's opportunity—with a final "look out now"—he backed out into Main Street. He made a neat turn, and accompanied by the throng of volunteers, he made his run through the village streets between lanes of frightened horses, alarmed women with babies, with the ruffles and flourishes of profane comment of drivers and passersby, all accompanied by the chanted monotone of his *claque*, the kids, "Get a hoss, Doc, open her up, Doc," while they ran pantingly alongside until they were winded.

Doc continued his dusty progress through the village streets at the break-neck speed of twenty miles per hour.

One warm day as Doc was making his bold journey down Main Street, he met the Supreme Crisis. That detached proton, Ashabel Hoffister Benton was making his regular passage from Swoort's Saloon to the Oosterhaut House with his mind firmly fixed on his duties and confident in his journey. Doc rounded the corner and fumbled frantically for the atomizer horn fixed to his dash.

He missed it and there was Ashabel silhouetted, frozen rigid in horror, against the brown road. He was squarely in Doc's sights, and the inevitable happened. One convulsive jackrabbit leap carried Ashabel almost clear, but the fender caught him and he spun into the ditch on his hands and knees. At this very instant Doc, unable to locate the horn, yelled in a hoarse unnatural voice "Look out Ash, ye damn fool."

Ash's reply was that of a sorrowing philosopher, "Whatsa matter, Doc?" he inquired as Doc passed.

"Are ye comin' back?"

It was the considered opinion of all of us that Ashabel had conducted himself as a true villager.

The Faith Healer:
A Villager's Story

That portion of New York State lying in the Finger Lake section between Lakes Seneca and Kenka will always be my home. My ancestors pioneered it. Its rolling lusty beauty, its deep glens, and blue bottomless lakes are now strangely reminiscent of Norway to me. Tourists roll through it by the thousands during the summer, but off the main highways it is little changed since early hardy Dutch settlers broke the virgin soil.

Its beauty is well advertised and appreciated, but the tough and earthly character of its people is not.

In 1912, prior to my departure on my first tour of foreign service, I returned home, and in search of news of the elder generation, stopped at the local hotel where the proprietor, as immutable a fixture as the spire on the Presbyterian church, was rocking quietly on his front porch, watching the daily peregrination of the population to the Post Office.

He suggested beer, for the day promised to be a hot one, and we repaired to his side porch to avoid inflicting local shock at such a flagrant violation of good taste as drinking beer in full view of the passing groups; this in spite of our certainty that each one knew pretty well what was happening.

We sipped our beer and settled down to that priceless pearl of leisurely conversation in which one turns the pearl from side to side examining it as to size and shape and enjoying the lambent fire and play of color.

I recognized many of the older people—a few I missed. I inquired after Charlie Trant. Bill stopped rocking. He looked through the fluttering maple leaves toward the street and sighed.

"Charlie," he said sadly "is dead—yeah, he died last fall." We both made appropriate clucking noises.

"Tell me about it," I suggested.

Bill resumed his slow comforting rocking. "Last fall, Harry, one of them Couay fellers came along..."

"Who?" I interrupted. "One of them Couay fellers." Bill said impatiently. "You know them fellers who heal people by sayin' 'day by day in every way, I'm gettin' better an' better.'" I nodded.

"Well, this particler feller rented my sample room. He set himself up a clinic there. That sample room is just off the bar, the exact place for a clinic thinks I. And dog it, the people did come. People I hadn't seen for years come down outa these hills and I could hear 'em a-saying 'day by day' till I got tired to death of it. Found myself sayin' it, too.

"Charlie Traut he came with the rest. Charlie had rheumatism so bad that fer nearly a year he'd walked on crutches. He usta come for his mail that way. Never missed a day rain or shine. In the winter and early spring he made it quite spry, but he was getting slower and slower. He usta stop here once in a while, although he'd had to give up beer, but he was still lotsa fun. I expect he heard these fellers in the sample room; anyway he become one of the regular customers."

Bill sipped his beer appreciatively. "I was sittin' right here one mornin'," he continued, "just like we are now, watchin' everybody come to get his mail, when Charlie walked out of that sample room. Yes, he walked out—no crutches—nothin', jest as straight as you are now. I was really s'prised, but I said nothin'. He seen me watchin' him tho', and in a loud voice you coulda heard clear over to the church yonder, he shouts 'Bill, I'm cured!' He started towards the steps there, and I heard him say 'day by day', and just then he tripped a little on the top step..."

Bill leaned forward pointing his glass at me, "an' he fell clear to the bottom of them stairs, and broke," said Bill in rising crescendo, "his goddamned neck!"

Neither of us smiled. It was too sad a subject.

Tragedy in New England

It was quite by chance that I came to live here in this little New Hampshire town. My wife had known and loved it from her early girlhood, and since I was brought up in the country, I appreciated her feelings about it.

In 1941 had to make a flight down into the Caribbean on some business for the military. We flew down in one of the Navy's seaplanes and made a landing on very rough water in the Gulf of Spain. It seemed that we were making it all right, when one of the wings caught a wave tip and we went round and round. The cockpit became well filled with water and I kept thinking, "My God, I meant to give my wife a power of attorney to handle all my property while this war was going on and I've forgotten it. If we make shore, the first thing I will do is to cable her one."

This I did.

When I returned to the States some months later, I found that I was part owner of a farm in New Hampshire. My wife was the other partner.

I, too, have become fond of the country and of the people who live by a sterner code than exists in most other areas. I like the way they face up to realities, and I admire their uncompromising integrity. Their wry humor is well known to the whole United States.

The most illustrative tale in our neighborhood has to do with a terrible tragedy in which the principal actor was a farmer who hanged himself from one of the beams in his barn. This occurrence shocked the whole neighborhood and they all hastened to do what they could to aid the grieving widow.

The coroner's jury, which was quickly assembled, met in the widow's kitchen. Since all the members of it had known the bereaved since they were boys, they were intent on making her testimony as painless as possible. The foreman of the jury put her at ease by saying, "Mrs. Jones, just tell the jury in your own words exactly what happened. Take your time and don't worry."

"Well," said the widow, "we got up in the mornin', same as usual; he lit his lantern, and went out to do the chores, an' I started gettin' breakfast. When breakfast was ready, I went out to call him, but they warn't no answer. I went on down to the barn," she paused, "an' I opened the door"—the jury braced itself—"an' thar he was, hanging by his neck from the rafters." She paused again, looked from one juror to the other, and concluded, "An' not a lick of work done."

This is the spirit of New England and I know it well. I married one of them.

Allies

For those readers who served in the Armed Forces circa WWII, Korea, and later on Viet Nam, this story is all too familiar. In WWII, fraternization with Germans during occupation days was taboo! Drunkenness was aggressively prosecuted by all Commands. Yet with American soldiers where there is a will, there is a way! Trying to keep young men away from pleasures of the flesh is like keeping bees from honey. The flow of "war brides" from Germany, France, England, Japan, Korea, and Viet Nam to the U.S. illustrates the futility of trying to curtail the forces of nature. It is too bad though that young men, particularly those of us in the U.S., free from the restraints of home celebrate their freedom by pushing the "envelope" when it came to drinking.

The Army films on V.D. (venereal disease) cooled the ardor a little bit, but as they say a "man's brain, lies below his belt buckle," unfortunately.

Allies

That the United States should ever have to fight a war without allies, is a grim thought indeed. In addition to the great help which we have reciprocally given and received from them in our wars, they have provided our troops with a great deal of amusing chatter; and I am certain that our troops have equally provided them with much of the same.

To the best of my knowledge and belief, we have had only one grumbling, grunting, and suspicious ally and it didn't take very long for him to disclose that he was only out to get what be could for himself. The Russian Bear has truly demonstrated the Chinese saying, so much appreciated by Joe Stillwell, that the higher climbs the monkey, the more he shows his nether parts.

It has seemed to me that in war, the French are closer to Americans than are the British and there is no known reason why this should be so unless, it is a matter of my personality.

It is interesting, indeed, to try to distinguish between the attitudes of America and Americans towards the two world wars in which we have been engaged in my active lifetime. Upon the outbreak of the first one, our Army, which had been rather apologetically endured by our upright citizenry, found itself hopelessly left behind by improvements in weapons (recently called weaponry, to make it sound respectable) and tactics to correspond. This situation led to the immediate dispatch of mission after mission to secure from our long suffering Allies, the know how to bring us back to some sort of standard where we might be able to cope.

Among the many advantageous imports through the missions (theirs and ours) in 1917 were details of instructors to serve with our training centers and show us how to meet terrible modern blows.

Our Air Service was just struggling to get its infant head off the pillow; our Navy, supposedly ready for its Mobilization Day mission, found itself deficient in torpedoes, antisubmarine devices, range finders, and calibers of guns: and our Army, which had the finest military rifle in the world as well as its recently designed, but not ready for issue, machine guns which, among other things, we had no modern artillery nor ammo for it.

So, the foreign instructors had much to do and very little to do it with. Nevertheless they made their mark!

Our system in training artillery included a tour at Fort Sill where each artillery brigade, prior to its departure overseas, could engage in firing problems on ranges ample for the full development of supporting tactical fires.

The foreign instructors were busy, indeed. Methods of precision adjustment, rolling barrages, concentrations and like fires were being encountered by our fledgling gunners for the first time. In the strained endeavors to assimilate this new data, many amenities were overlooked. The young English instructors who insisted that each of the younger American officers, their charges, appeared clean shaven in the morning, as opposed to being clean shaven in the evening when each wanted to get to town quickly to visit his wife or some other gal, while generally reviled were obeyed without dissent, for the First World War was a real crusade against Satan and his forces, then concentrated, strong, and efficient.

The young French artillery officers, less attentive to such matters, were more in favor. There were two of them at Sill, both Captains. Both proceeded to grow huge and luxurious beards. In addition, one sported a moustache. It was a beautiful golden color and when spread its real wing tips reached the ears of its proud wearer. He was instantly and unanimously christened "Handle Bar Pete." He was immensely proud of his nickname and was well aware that it was bestowed in all good nature and was evidence that he had been admitted to a real American "ferreting and *égalité."*

His compatriot passed up the moustache, but developed a beard of the General Grant type—a wonderful growth to behold. He looked so dignified behind the beard, that no one had the heart to bestow a nickname and was generally hailed by his proper name Captain Michael. These two worthies were, indeed, fully occupied for we were getting our artillery and ammunition from France and were making the acquaintance of the justly famous French 75 and the French names *Plateau* and *tambour* which went with it.

It was inevitable that among the many missions which our War Department had sent overseas, there should be at least one from the YMCA, or similar institution, and that it should return to the States. I presume that in Washington, not being able to think of anything more useful for it to do, someone had made up his mind to send it to Fort Sill where an artillery brigade was completing its training prior to its departure to the Theater of Operations.

When two men from this mission of the YMCA reported to the Brigade Commander, they brought with them a message from the Chief of Staff to the effect that they were to be given a chance to talk to the Personnel Officer of the Brigade to tell them of the conditions existing in France which would affect the morale of the men—and that he should render a report on the value of the information they put out.

The CO was a little bit embarrassed about the talk. All the time available had been set up for much needed training and he well knew the eagerness with which the officers of his command started for town in the evening. Still the period immediately after dinner in the Officers' Mess was the most appropriate, and, however reluctantly, he set that time for the talk.

The CO had both the YMCA men at his table and since they were in civilian clothes, none of the youngsters suspected that they were to talk. As soon as dinner was fairly concluded, the CO rose, and pounded on his glass until there was some semblance of order, and announced the fact that they were fortunate tonight to have as guests Mr. Brown and Mr. Green who had been sent down by the War Department to tell them of the conditions in France and the general rules under which our forces, already there, were working. Before the sodden reaction of the panting off-to-towners could make itself manifest, he concluded with "May I introduce Mr. Brown."

The English artillery instructors had been present from the first and registered intent. Now the two French *artilleurs* entered the dining room and, like true Frenchmen, proceeded to start their dinners quietly, but with a degree of concentration sufficient to render them impervious to outside influences. Each had carefully tucked his napkin under his chin and over his beard, and now ate with enjoyment, and perforce, listened to Mr. Brown's carefully prepared talk.

Mr. Brown was certainly not at home with such a simple audience. Still, they listened intently to the picture he drew. He stated that it had been decided that in cooperation with the Military Police of the French and American armies, as well as the local *gendarmerie*, those rules which were at the basis of discipline must be rigidly enforced. These included practically everything: no visiting Paris except by quota determined by the CO of the city; no drinking—not even the wine of the country; great care in not doing, or saying, anything to mar the good will of the countrymen or the other Allies. But above all, since drinking was at the bottom of violations of such rules, there was an absolute, repeat absolute, ban on any drinking of alcoholic beverages. He then sat down.

His audience now had subsided to absolute quiet. Not a sound. The CO seemed a little uneasy and hastened to get on with his work by introducing to the still stunned Personnel Officer, the next on the list of speakers, Mr. Green.

Mr. Green arose and took up the tale from the point where Mr. Brown had laid it down. There were many American officers, he opined, who were looking forward to going to France, with the idea of drinking all the French wines and brandies and other liquors, for which, principally due to lack of understanding of the French, we Americans had assumed the French to be famous. As Mr. Brown had so well put it, that was definitely out.

But there was another thing, which he felt impelled to call to the attention of the younger officers. There were also many Americans who were looking forward to going to France because they thought that there they could find many girls who could make them forget really why they had come to the Theater of Operations.

Need he be more specific? Well, that was out.

Just as in the cases of those who drank in Paris and other places, all the authorities, Allied and civilian, but principally the Military Police, had orders that all military personnel caught walking with women of questionable character, were to be sent or taken to 10 Rue Sainte Anne (a sort of an American hell) and held for trial either in their units or in Paris itself.

Now the CO became really uneasy. He felt the morale of his Brigade, which he had worked so long to establish, ebbing away slowly, but certainly. In desperation, he rose and looked around, for inspiration. His eye took in the two French instructors now sitting with cupped ears, supper completely neglected, and terribly concentrated on the speaker.

The CO said hopefully "Perhaps one of our French instructors would care to comment. You, Colonel?"

And Handle Bar Pete stood up, his napkin which had slipped down around his neck making a nice background for his golden beard. "Yes," he said loudly, "yes I would." Then without waiting for more encouragement from the CO, "What ees this? In France you can not drink ze wine. You can not come to Paris. You can not walk wiz ze girl? Well, zhentlemen, who eez it to prevent?"

His voice rose to a shrill indignant pitch. "Well, by Gar, zhentlemen does ze interfere wiz your pleasure, you KEEL him." With that he subsided.

The applause nearly tore the tin roof off the overheated mess hall. I have always thought that the CO started the applause. I have often wondered what he put in that report on the effectiveness of the speeches.

Mussoorie

July 30, 1944

I have finally seen something of what people rave about in India. It was so unusual I am sure that I can't describe it adequately.

Last week several of us went to Dehradun and Mussoorie (about 175 miles north of Delhi); look them up on the map. Dehradun is a beautiful summer resort, there are many in "the hills," but Mussoorie is a bit of *Heaven*. You go six miles beyond Dehradun to get on the road to Mussoorie. As you look up from that point, you can see the homes and hotels, etc., six thousand feet straight up. The road winds around, and I mean winds, for twenty-two miles—somewhat like going up Pikes Peak, but the road twists a great deal more, and the hair pin curves are much more dangerous. Only one-way traffic at a time is permitted.

The brilliant green foliage is interspersed with waterfalls, wild white and yellow lilies, and many strange native flowers, all beautiful. There are thousands of vivid green terraced rice paddies, baboons, monkeys, parrots and birds of all sizes and colors. You hear strange music and suddenly come upon flute playing goat herders. This queer trip, as you go up and up, during most of which twenty-two miles you hold on to your seat, scared to death dozen times; in a command car, almost as big as a truck, the weight of which added to our worry as there were already several delays due to heavy rains causing land slides which had to be dug out.

We were stopped at least four times to register, show our credentials, pay toll, and have our license number checked and double checked. We left our car about one mile from the top as the grade is too steep. We got out and were carried in a swinging seat to the top by four coolies; there were dozens of shouting applicants for the job.

The top is Mussoorie—Shangri-La, if there ever was one—the town extends for about three miles; only one street along the ridge of the mountain no wider than the Sky Line Drive in Virginia at its narrowest point. All this is on top of one of the foothills of the Himalayas, which disappear in the clouds close by to the north. There are lots of clouds that hang low and travel fast, lots of rain, but sunny most of the time; very quick changes, reminded me of the fact that an umbrella is the most used stick in your golf bag at the Broadmoor Links in Colorado.

In walking around you have a feeling of being in an airplane, or on the deck of a huge steamer, particularly when the clouds go by so fast. The beauty of the whole setting is unbelievable. Delightful hotels, residences, shops and nightclubs, and without a doubt one of the nicest crowds of people, many English and few Americans, you could find anywhere. There are Newabs, Nazims, and Maharajas who live in splendor such as Metro-Goldwyn-Mayer never dreamed of.

One evening as we sat on the veranda of our part of the hotel, we listened to the weirdest singing coming from a temple about a hundred yards away. At first we didn't like it, but soon it sounded like an old Southern granny's lullaby. It never seemed to stop and easily outran a twenty-four player Capehart before we moved on.

One night we visited a very elaborate nightclub. The music was modern and excellent. Our table was situated next to the Nawab of Rampur. His party of about forty was served by his private waiters, with his own wine stewards, bodyguards, etc., who were a sight to behold in their many hued costumes, as picturesque as his guests. Through a little wire pulling, and a few properly placed rupees, we were served the same food as they, and the Colony Restaurant in New York could take a few lessons from them. The Newab and his *memsahib* had arrived in a Victoria like this: shiny black lacquer and gold body rubber-tired wheels—6 coolies in front and 6 behind, pulling and pushing on the handlebars fore and aft. It was a real 12-cylinder job. The coolies were all decked out in splendid gold brocade uniforms, but barefooted, of course. Guests arrived in similar contraptions, but with only 8 or 10 "cylinders" instead of 12.

I am told that there are several other summer resorts similar to Mussoorie, but as yet I haven't seen them and I doubt if any can compare more favorably. I always suspected that I was sybarite, Mussoorie confirmed it.

The contrast between this concentration of wealth and the unbelievable poverty of the country and villages you go through to get there is something that is hard to forget. En route through the country the cattle, *all-sacred*, almost stop traffic; sleep in the road—in fact, practically with the natives. There are literally two hundred million cattle, which, because of their uselessness, always have and always will, I guess, help pauperize four hundred million people.

In the villages it looks like the people don't even have the necessities of life. Everything is most primitive, mud huts, etc. Sanitation is just nonexistent. We passed several grain and cereal stores, for instance, which had wheat, rice, oats, and rye all displayed for sale in neat piles right on the naked ground. The sun is hot, the sacred cattle stand unmolested all around, the dogs bark, and the stench reaches to high heaven. There were dozens of children. The only buildings that look like anything are the temples. They are most numerous and gaudy, and seem to be the Stork Club and the local country store all combined and no doubt will ever continue to dominate the social and economic life and customs of these people with their age-old and deep-rooted religions. The natives, however, apparently love life, which bountifully offers them an average life expectancy of twenty-seven years and an average per capita annual income of seven dollars.

Part II

Our Blessed Country

Introduction

The stories in this section of the book run the gamut of truly historical and personal events witnessed by my family from 1807 through the Civil War in 1865, and others through 1946. It gives the reader a sense of the character of our nation as it grew in that period of time and thus the title.

The characters are John Malony; General Robert E. Lee; President of Georgetown College; Leander, a freed Union Army prisoner, who had to walk hundreds of miles home; Maj. General King a prisoner at the Japanese prison camp at Bataan; P.I. Major General Bruce, who took the time and trouble to speak with the son of his waitress in a remote small restaurant.

Included in the narratives is a riveting story of events in 1807 of a court marshal of my great great uncle, James Barron, and his subsequent duel in which he killed Commodore Steven Decatur, his accuser. Also, you will read of the Post WWII War Criminal Trials in which unknown atrocities are revealed.

Sinking Of The *Chesapeake* (1807)

The sinking of the *Chesapeake* was one of many events leading to War of 1812 with the British. James Barron, my great great uncle, and Stephen Decatur, both Commodores, highest naval rank, are rivals for command responsibilities in the U.S. Navy.

The story centers around Steven Decatur's efforts to disgrace James Barron and his untimely end. The crew members of James Barron, by chance met Stephen Decatur who had been calling upon a lady of dubious reputation. The meeting resulted in a barrage of insults heaped upon Steven Decatur by Barron's crew. James Barron failed to discipline his crew for the incident, thus showing further disrespect.

The British Navy gang pressed American seamen to enlist in the British Navy. By British Law, desertion was classified as a crime punishable by hanging. The British ship *Leopard* encountered the U.S. ship *Chesapeake* which had the U.S. deserters from the gang pressed British crews on board. The ensuing fire fight resulted in the disability of the *Chesapeake* and the Court Marshalling of Commodore James Barron, who was a passenger.

In 1807 there was substantial British Naval presence in U.S. waters under the command of Lord Halifax. As a regular practice, the British would kidnap ("gang press") American young men from the bars along the seaboard and force them to sign with the British Navy for a period of time as sailors.

The British had "recruited" three young Americans from a pub in Norfolk, Virginia where they had been drinking. Later, the three "recruits" escaped from the ship to which they had been assigned and were declared "deserters" by the British. Thus, by British law, they could be hanged for desertion despite their U.S. citizenship.

The British then demanded that the deserters who were American citizens be turned over to them for disciplinary actions, possibly hanging. The U.S. government refused. The accused seamen joined the U.S. ship *Chesapeake*.

Commodore James Barron, at the time, was the Commodore of the U.S. Navy, headquartered in Norfolk, Virginia. His principal rival was Stephen Decatur who had also risen through the ranks to Commodore. It should be noted that the father of James Barron was James Barron, referred to as "the elder" who was formerly Commodore of all U.S. Naval vessels. Commodore James Barron came aboard the *Chesapeake* and was barely out to sea when he encountered the Leopard.

Stephen Decatur had served in the Mediterranean in 1799 under James Barron, the Elder, and was a keen rival of the younger James Barron for Navy promotions.

The incident to which Decatur refers occurred when a group of young officers serving under James Barron, were gathered in Norfolk and were en route to a local tavern when they encountered Stephen Decatur, who was either in route to, or from, the residence of a young lady of dubious reputation. What occurred was a series of rude remarks made to Decatur and apparent disrespect to his rank, his person, and possibly his family. Although James Barron had no participation in this affair, he took no action against his officers. This led to Decatur's actions against Barron in the "*Chesapeake* Affair" which resulted in Barron's removal by Court Martial from all active command for five years without pay as noted in the material to follow. He had been court marshalled on the charges of not having the *Chesapeake* properly readied for possible encounters with the British fleet; for surrendering "too quickly" although he argued that he was substantially out gunned by the British ship. According to accounts, only one gun of the *Chesapeake* was fired; four crew members were killed, and eighteen wounded. The British boarded Barron's ship and removed the three "deserters" plus one for good measure. Barron was not charged with cowardice, but with neglecting to have the ship properly readied for encounters, properly stowed supplies, and limited munitions on board.

James Barron then accepted an equivalent as Admiral from the French Navy where he served for five years. In 1920 he challenged Stephen Decatur to a duel because of Decatur's repeated deprecatory remarks which he felt were keeping him from a new command. Decatur was a hero of the War of 1812, and Barron felt stood in his way constantly with his derision. The duel was attended by Commodore Bainbridge. Although wounded in the leg, Barron's shot delivered the killing blow to Decatur who passed a few hours after the duel.

Barron headed up the Navy Yard in Philadelphia and continued to work diligently for the Navy despite never having a command again. One of his contributions to the Navy was his recommendation that ships be iron clad, an idea that historically speaks for itself.

John Malony's Letter To The Hon. Ryland Fletcher (1862)

John Malony, my grandfather, ran away from his small home in upstate New York as a teenager from a stepmother who actively disliked him and beat him constantly. He had lost his mother at age seven when his formal schooling ended. In spite of this handicap, he was able to win a position as a clerk in the office of a New York State Congressman in his Senate office in Washington, D.C. Later, as a student at Georgetown College, he graduated as a doctor.

The story which follows describes his successful efforts as a young man to bring aid and comfort as a volunteer to the 40,000 Union soldiers who were dead or dying on the battlefield of the Second Battle Of Bull Run.

One of the interesting aspects of John Malony's account is the personal courtesy afforded by both General Robert E. Lee and William T. Sherman to John Malony, a young teen-aged boy who was on an errand of mercy.

John's letter to Ryland Fletcher of U.S. Pension Office in Washington, D.C. offers a unique insight into the cowardly actions of government workers who were brought in to help the dead, dying and grievously wounded on the battlefield, but deserted instead.

Pension Office
Washington D.C. July 9th 1862

Hon. Ryland Fletcher
Dear Sir,

Your communication of the 23rd *ultimo*[4] was duly received, but owing to being called away from the duties of the office to that of nursing to the wounded upon the battlefield I have failed to respond until now. For your kind reply please accept my most sincere and grateful thanks. For your good advice I cannot thank you sufficiently; it is to me a pillar of fire by night and a monument by day to guard me safely through all temptations with which all young men in this City are so constantly beset, never while memory clings to me shall I ever fail to remember and appreciate your advice. I have been upon the far famed battlefield of Manassas and

---

[4] Last month

thinking perhaps that it will interest you I will try and give your account of my experience in Dixie.

One week ago last Saturday a dispatch came from the Secretary of War to the Secretary of the Interior requesting him to ask the clerks of his Department to volunteer to act as nurses to the wounded soldiers and all that would go prepare to go immediately, and along with the dispatch came the rumor that were 18,000 killed and wounded soldiers laying upon the bloody fields of Bull Run and Manassas, this was told to us when the dispatch was read. Of course we all promptly responded and as we had but one hour to get ready in "then and there were hurrying to and fro." There was a special train ordered to take us up to Fairfax Station and from there ambulances were to take us to the field. I got into the cars precisely at 5 o'clock the time designated for us to staff and found the train crowded with clerks and heads of Bureaus, and prominent citizens. We all had plenty of lint and bandages for immediate use and the relief committee had plenty of Cordials and stimulant to give to the wounded. We waited and waited impatiently at the station for the cars to start and it was eleven o'clock before the cars started away from Washington.

We arrived at Alexandria about 10 o'clock and proceeded very slowly from there to Fairfax Station expecting every movement to run off the track or hear the crack of the sentinel's rifle. We had to part with part of the train about halfway as it was so heavy, but a Locomotive came up and pushed it on behind us. We reached Fairfax Station about 5 o'clock in the morning and found it guarded by a small detachment of Cavalry, but found no ambulances that we had expected to take us to the field and what was worse nobody knew positively where the Battlefield was. About 8 o'clock a telegraph came from the Secretary of War ordering the Engineer to take us as far as Bull Run Bridge and from there we might walk to the battlefield. Our company now was about one thousand strong and we all had to find Bull Run. There were many laughable incidents that occurred. I started for Bristol Station where General Banks was fighting the enemy and found I could not get inside the lines. Standing upon a hill as I was I could distinctly see and hear shells bursting high in the air. This was on Sunday about 2 o'clock and by this time two-thirds of our company had "skedaddled" back to Fairfax Station and took the first train to Washington; others had been put back to Centerville; at last all had gone but a friend of mine, a Vermonter, as we stood anxiously awaiting trying to learn something of the movement of our Army. We heard General Banks blowing up his ammunition; a medical officer at this time rode up and informed us that Banks was retreating towards Centerville and that we had better go along with his trains that had now appeared upon the brow of a hill looking towards Bristol Station. We turned our faces towards Centerville, which was almost twelve miles distant, and walked towards there over one of the muddiest roads that Virginia can boast of.

About halfway there we found a Hospital by the roadside, which was evident with wounded; they were being put into ambulances and taken towards Centerville. I arrived at Centerville about 6 o'clock and found a considerable portion of our Army encamped there. I and my friend found lodging upon the floor of an old colored woman's house and would have slept soundly had not a small pig (a curiosity in the country here) intruded upon our positions and disrupted our rights to the floor; after a short, but fierce, engagement we resumed in putting ourselves out of his reach. We remained upon this field two days and one night. All night I slept under a tree in an orchard with hundreds wounded laying around me; the night was cold and it rained hard, but I rolled myself up in a blanket with a "big Zouave" and being very tired was soon in the land of nod. When I awoke next day there was still plenty of work to be-done and nobody to do it. I went again to work with a will trying to alleviate the sufferings of the poor fellows, but our stock of provisions had nearly given out and hundreds of poor fellows were obliged to go hungry - that had gone on two or three days already –at night we started under a flag of truce for our lines stopping however to parole the wounded prisoners. We reached Centerville about 7 o clock in the evening and found that our troops had evacuated the position and had fallen back towards Falls Church that was occupied by a regiment of Rebel Cavalry. We were sent under guard to the Headquarters of General Lee, so we arrived at his Headquarters about 12 o'clock in the night. We stayed there about two hours when General Jackson gave us a pass to our lines; while there I was introduced to the notorious individual who received me very kindly and courteously. He was standing by a campfire with a long military cloak wrapped around him and as I expressed a wish to see him to one of his couriers he very kindly took me up and introduced me to him. Upon my way I saw General Lee at Fairfax Courthouse.

When we awoke in the morning we managed to procure some coffee and biscuits. The biscuit I think must have been made upon the principle of a lighted candle, that "the longer it lives the shorter it grows," for the longer we chewed the larger it grew. I would recommend them to be introduced into the Commissary Department as one mouthful would be sufficient to feed any man. To throw aside jesting and proceed this day I got into an ambulance and entered the enemies lines under a flag of truce; we were received very courteously and shown to the Battlefield which was about ten miles distant; we arrived upon the field and such a sight as there met my gaze I shall never forget. Wounded men by scores were laying out under a hot burning sun with their arms and limbs shattered and torn off in a most horrible style, and to add to all the honor and untold misery, the stench was in some places insufferable owing to the piles of mangled remains of both man and horse which were decaying under the influences of a hot Southern sun.

This was no time to shirk, there were more than 40 civilians from Washington and we took a stretcher and under charge of a surgeon proceeded to the left wing of the Army and commenced to carry the wounded to the side of Bull Run Stream under the shade of large trees. We then fed them and gave them stimulants and bound up their wounds as well as possible under the circumstances.

John Malony

John Malony's Letter To Provost At Georgetown College (1864)

> In 1864 the Civil War has ended and John Malony served as an administrator and was seeking an education at Georgetown College to better himself (he was basically uneducated coming from a broken family). This story is the letter he wrote to Georgetown seeking admittance.
>
> John was working his way through college. His brothers gave him a little money every month and John paid the rest.

Washington, D.C.
October, 1864

Sir,

Asking pardon for intruding on your time and patience, I would most earnestly request you to give these few lines your favorable consideration. I desire an education, but unfortunately am unable to receive one for want of funds to defray the necessary expenses. I was born poor and at the age of seven was taken from School and since then I have received no instructions but those gathered in the rude school of experience. It was the dying wish of my mother that I should be brought up in the Catholic religion but bigotry had taught me to abhor the name and I have been negligent enough to almost forget the rudiments of the faith though my mother labored to impress upon my youthful mind. I have latterly endeavored to learn the truth. How often have I wished as I strolled by the College Building that I was within its peaceful walls than to acquire some of its accomplishments?

Indeed Sir, I have earnestly longed to become a Scholar. I have now reached the age of Twenty, and I feel that all the hopes for an education, with which I had comforted myself are fast fading away. I believe that if I could go to School one year more I would be taught sufficiency's for many professions of life. A brother tells me that he would allow me a certain sum every month. I think that I could pay the Tuition every month in advance could I not make some arrangement of that kind as I have not the whole sum. If you could aid and assist me by advice, or action, you would confer a favor that would always be remembered. An early answer would be thankfully received. Again asking pardon for this intrusion but trust in that it will not be in vain.

I remain most respectfully and anxiously your obedient servant.

John W. Malony

General King's farewell to US Prisoners—Unsung Hero (1942)

Address of General King to American prisoners at Camp O'Donnell concentration camp, Philippine Islands, on or about May, 1942

> General King's farewell to fellow U.S. prisoners of war at the Japanese POW Camp at Camp O'Donnell, Philippine Islands. Although he was not related to our family, we had known him and his children for decades, and his concern for his imprisoned soldiers and his personal bravery at Corregidor when he was forced to surrender to the Japanese, will always stay in my mind as a fine man and a brave person.

Orientation

General King had acquired *sub rosa* information that he and other senior officers would shortly be moved by the Japanese from Camp O'Donnell to another place of confinement and made the following talk to all the survivors of Bataan (8,600 men approximately) prior to his departure on the 10th of May.

The General's objective in making this talk was to try to improve the morale of those wretched survivors and to give them a mission to tend to tie them together in a spirit of camaraderie for the long hard pull during the long years he knew they would be prisoners.

As the Japanese had given him strict orders against assemblies of any sort, the General walked about standing amongst small groups repeating his words until all had heard.

Address

General King said substantially as follows:

> I have reason to believe that I shall be sent to another Camp and before I leave I want to tell you how magnificent you

133

have been. You fought valorously as long as you were able and when the end comes, I want you to know that I do not consider that you surrendered. It was I who surrendered you.

General King continued with adjurations of hope for the future and prison camp conduct, and concluded by saying:

While we are no longer a fighting force, we continue to have a mission. Our mission now is that we shall one day go home, and so as I say goodbye, I ask everyone of you, officer, non-commissioned officers, and men alike to conduct yourselves in all your relations with each other so that as many of you as possible have the opportunity to go home.

As General King walked away from these little groups, he was barely able to keep himself under control, for as he left, men made no attempt to keep back the tears: some in desperate stages of malaria and dysentery, tried to pull themselves up from the ground along the side of the building in an effort to salute him while crying like children.

Major General A.G. Tisdalle Jr., Inf.
HQ Fla. Mil. Diet.

A Boy's Letter to His Mother (1943)

I knew General Bruce, the subject of this letter, when I was growing up at Fort McNair in Washington. I like this letter for several reasons: the first is the insight it offers in the mind of a young private in the Army from a rural area, as green as grass but who shone as bright as a new penny through his naivety—a good man through and through. Secondly, General Bruce, who was waited upon by his mother, a waitress in a crossroads rural restaurant, took the pains to look up the son and spend time with him—a small bit of kindness that will undoubtedly stay with the young soldier for the rest of his life.

In General Bruce's case it clearly illustrates the old Southern maxim—*One never flies so high that he doesn't have to poop on the ground.*

(Undated, but written sometime in April 1943)

Hello *Udder*:

Boy, was I surprised! I came off walking post on guard the other day and the charge of quarters told me to pull off my leggins and put on my jacket and report to Battalion Headquarters. I didn't know what to think. A lot of things came into my mind, but you guess that I didn't get it right. I thought that I did something wrong, or maybe something good. I couldn't think of anything good that I had done lately, so I just kept wondering and went down to battalion headquarters to find out what was wanted.

When I went in I asked our company clerk if I was wanted there, and he said, "Yes, you are going to see the 'General!'" I thought he was kidding me, but then he told me to go and see LT Black (he was Battalion Personnel Officer).

I reported to him, and he asked me if I knew of any reason why I should go to see the General. Of course, I told him that I didn't, but then he told me, "Well, that's where you are going." He told me to straighten my tie, and not to forget to report in proper manner. He then told me also where to go.

Well, I lit out for the building that LT Black told me about and walked in. When I went in I saw on my right a sign that said "Information."

I asked at that desk who should I see to get to see the General, and they told me to go into an office to my left. I went into it and a Tech. Sergeant came in and told me to repeat my story.

After I had done that he showed me the way to a Colonel's office (G-2 for investigation). I answered his questions and he told me there must be some mistake, that the General did not want to see me, but he sent me down to see a Captain (Adjutant). I told the Captain what had been told to me at Battalion HQ. He told me to wait there a minute.

In a short bit he came back and told me to follow him. Well, I did, and he escorted me to a waiting room. I waited about five minutes while some Captains went in and came out. Then I went in, I can still imagine how awful I looked: dirty tie; dirty jacket; shoes shined, but black as tar, with broken strings; my face was shaved, but it could have been better; and to top it all my hair looked like a rat's nest.

It was so unexpected though and I couldn't imagine what the General could be wanting to see me for, and the time I had to get ready was *none*.

But anyway, when I walked in I knew who it would be for there is only one General in our camp and he is "General Bruce." But to make sure I cut my eyes left to see him. I reported and he told me to have a seat.

After I sat down, he asked me where I was born. I told him, and then he asked me if I liked it there. I said, "Yes, Sir, very much." And then he told that he had been to Atlanta by plane and while there he had seen my mother. He said you had waited on him while there. It surprised me so much that I couldn't say one word. The only thing I could do was smile.

He said, "She told me what a fine boy you were."

I still couldn't say anything. (*Udder*, I'm telling you the truth, I was nervous, excited, and surprised so much it's a wonder I remember what he said to me at all). And then he mentioned the $100 I sent home, and wondered out loud if had won it gambling. That was the only thing I could answer to talk about, and that only one sentence, and here is how that sentence went: "I'll admit, Sir, that I gamble every once in awhile, but I didn't win that money gambling." He said, "I was only kidding you there."

Honest, I don't remember what was said next, but I do remember when I left he told me to be sure and write you and tell you I had talked to him. And when I left I saluted and said, "Yes, Sir. I'll do that, Sir."

Whether he wanted me to go then, or whether he wanted me to stay and talk awhile longer I don't know.

Most likely I'll live the rest of my life and I'll never have anything to happen to me as that happened. I'm still wondering about it. I believe I left before I should have, and I must have seemed rude or something like that the way I left.

When I went in I didn't have any idea what would happen. I was scared, surprised, pleased, and everything. And, *Udder*, when he told me you had waited on him, I just couldn't think of anything to say and so I didn't ask him how you were, or if you seemed well, or anything. Probably the reason was that today he is one of the most important men in the world; commanding the only Tank Destroyer School and Camp in the world; setting up new ideas and tactics that even now are being used in North Africa. You may not think it is anything to have something happen to you like that, but I know there are only a few soldiers who are called to talk to the Commanding General and have him say that he saw your mother back in your home town (I know I left too soon, now. I didn't ask one question), and you know he called you there for that reason.

Well, I missed that chance to talk, but I say it was all my fault, and maybe if ever another time comes up like that to say, or to put it correctly—be able to say *something*.

Udder, tell me how you happened to know where he was from, and how he found out I was here.

With that I'll close, hoping you all are O.K., and sending you all my love.

Love to you all,

Neal

Leander's Story (1944)

> Leander was small town boy born in Indiana and was related to me through my family in the Civil War years.

Leander Spencer and his brother volunteered to serve in the Union Army and were captured and imprisoned by Confederate forces after several years of combat. As Leander's brother died of measles, Leander was assigned to Andersonville prison, truly a hell hole; perhaps the most notorious of that time with poor food; no medical care; and disgusting sanitary conditions, which caused the mortality rates to soar.

After the surrender of the Army of Virginia by Robert E. Lee at Appomatox, Union prisoners were released and told to go home; most just walked. It is easy to envision: emancipated and wounded soldiers struggling through small villages on their way; it must have been a heart tugging sight. I am sure that the people in these small towns and villages offered food and shelter to these soldiers as best they could. As groups of soldiers marched through Leander's town, Leader was not to be seen. After looking in vain, Leander's father selected a wounded, dirty, half-starved soldier and took him to his home and started to feed him dinner. As the dinner progressed, Leander finally cried out "Pa, it's me, Leander, don't you recognize me?" No one did.

Stephen Ross's Story (1945)

> Stephen Ross was a Jewish boy from Poland who is seized by the Nazi's and held at Dachau Prison for five years until freed by the U.S. Army in 1945. His tale is heartbreaking and heroic.

(On behalf of the American Legion—founded Citizens Flag Alliance)

I came to America as an orphan on April 10, 1948, and I became a naturalized citizen of the United States on May 3, 1953.

I came from the place of gas chambers, fire, ashes, and chaos to my adopted country. The American people embraced me and took me under their wing, and gave me an opportunity to grow and prosper so that I could become one of them. I am proud to live free in this generous society.

Fifty years ago, American soldiers saved me from the hell of Dachau. They nursed me back to health and restored my will to live. Yet, what I remember most about my liberation is my tears being spilled on a small American flag. From that day to this, my love for our flag has never faltered.

My story begins in 1940. When I was 9 years old, the Germans took me from my home in Krasnik, Poland.

For five years, I was a prisoner of the Nazis in ten death camps, where I saw thousands of men, women and children brutally murdered and starved, or worked to death by the Nazi's death machine.

I lived on breadcrumbs, sawdust, human remains, and one small prayer for redemption or death—whichever was quicker.

My prayers were answered on April 29, 1945, when I was liberated from Dachau by the 42nd and 45th Infantry Divisions of the U.S. 7th Army. We were nursed for several days by these war-weary, but compassionate men and women, until we had enough strength to travel to Munich for additional medical attention.

As we walked ever so slowly and unsteadily toward our salvation, a young American tank commander, whose name I have never known, jumped off his tank to help us in whatever way he could.

When he saw that I was just a young boy, despite my gaunt appearance, he stopped to offer me comfort and compassion. He gave me his own food. He touched my withered body with his hands and his heart. His kindness installed in me a will to live, and I fell at his feet and shed my tears unsparingly which he dried with a cloth, which he left with me. As he left I looked down at the cloth with which he had lovingly dried my tears and it was the American Flag. This flag and for which it stands, will always be part of me, and in my prayers I will always bless our country and our flag.

War Crimes (1946)

> As the war ended in 1945 and Allies seized prisons camps in their sector, unspeakable crimes and abuses in prisons were revealed. The following story is one instance among many.

The War Crimes Trial for those accused of being responsible for issuing orders culminating in the Malmedy Massacre was conducted at Dachau, Germany. Reminders that the compound had been a concentration camp were still visible, while I was there in July 1946 and commanded the 2nd Battalion, 60th Inf. Regt., 9th Inf. Div. Soldiers of my battalion guarded the POW cage occupied by the former concentration camp personnel now on trial while they were in the court room for War Crimes.

I visited the courtroom at least once a day to observe my men and be assured of their alertness and proper demeanor. While in the courtroom, I had the opportunity to observe the trial and the actions and reactions of the German officers and, as I remember, some Sergeants accused of War Crimes. I observed their behavior when they sat there, with some looking very bored with the whole business, or when they were called to testify. We, of the Guard Battalion, had to ensure that the boredom did not affect us, nor our men, to the extent of becoming careless. The trial progressed very slowly, as every word of every question or comment had to be carefully translated into English. From a spectator point of view, it soon became very dull.

Those on trial were seated on a bare wooden bleacher, as if they were at a football game instead of on trial for their lives! The defendants had been SS troops, from "Sepp" Dietrich, the Commanding General, down to the sergeants. One particular individual always sat straight and erect with dignity and poise befitting a Colonel. He was alert and scarcely seemed to relax. Had one not known of the crime of which he had been accused, one might wonder why such a fine looking man as he was there at all. I learned he was COL Joachim Peiper, SS *Standartenführer*[5], Commander of the 1st SS Regiment of the 1st SS Division in the attack at the

---

[5] Highest field rank officer

Bulge and expected by the Germans to roll over the troops in the Ardennes. In 1946, he looked far different from the COL Peiper I recently saw in a recent issue of the "Retired Officer" showing him sprawled on a chair with a large number on a placard hanging from around his neck.

"How About Prisoners?"

During one session, a Lieutenant, a tank platoon leader, was being very carefully questioned about the orders he had received for the attack in the Ardennes. The prosecutor closely questioned the Lieutenant about every detail of his orders: the objective; the date and time of departure; phase lines; supply and resupply; location of food, ammunition and gasoline resupply points; boundaries; supporting units; and just about everything the prosecutor could think of. The questions and answers took a very long time and the answers became automatic and mechanical as the Lieutenant concentrated on the content of his replies. The prosecutor sounded sympathetic…as he asked about the orders for the treatment and evacuation of German wounded, and the Lieutenant mechanically explained their system.

The prosecutor innocently asked "How about the U.S. Prisoners?" The Lieutenant replied, "Our orders were to shoot them." The prosecutor started to rise to emphasize that comment. His co-workers grabbed him by the seat of his pants and yanked him down, with "No further questions," while the Lieutenant's remark still rang in everyone's ears.

COL Peiper showed no emotion and looked over our heads, apparently uncomfortable, but not surprised.

Postscript

Peiper was sentenced to death, the sentence changed to life imprisonment. He was released from prison in December 1956 and went back to France to live.

Peiper worked as a translator, this man who had been a full colonel by age twenty-nine; the man who was found guilty of war crimes. Peiper died in 1976 when his home was fire bombed. Those who did the bombing were never identified.

Part III

Postscript

Poems My Father Wrote

Included are a small number of poems, some humorous and a few which contain life lessons which any reader would do well to follow.

The Morning Mail

Here in Virginia, these snappy fall mornings
Are gaudy with color and cold weather warnings.
An' down Shirley Highway, a-speedin' to hell an' gone
Come cars by the thousands en route to the Pentagon,
For the pre-conference conference at quarter till eight
Each driver damns traffic—can't afford to be late.
And I turn back to breakfast—ambition unfired—
Raising paeans of thanksgiving that I am retired
THEN ALONG COMES THE MAIL.

Oh buy a nice Virginia ham
(peanut fed and tough as hell)
Came from Admiral Dewey's stores
As black as any five inch shell.

Woody says "Please pay your bill"
House-a-Mercy seeks your aid.
Unwed mothers need you still.
Sale at Hecht's on Putz Pomade.

Fill that basket. Read to front
With the junk marked "Occupants"
Made the postman grain an' grunt
Raised the price of postage stamps.

Woody says "Get out of stocks."
Value Line says "Hold em tight."

Steel strike man head full of rocks
Investors ante up for strikes.

U.S. wants third quarter tax
Bank cries out, "You're overdrawn"
Cannot like these old wise cracks
'For she get here Christmas gone.

So, here in Virginia, the leaves are all falling
And Nature bedecked all in colors is calling.
The mocking bird sings on his hickory limb
He whistles to me and I whistle to him
And the mailman is coming, my mail *must* be read
So I pick it up neatly
    AND GO BACK TO BED.

The strange Australian fauna yields

The strange Australian fauna yields
An absolute ringer for W.C. Fields.
He never drinks water. Like other folks here
He has to make do on a diet of beer.

He's born very little, an inch more or less
Then back in Ma's pouch for six months I confess.
And the ladies adore him and hug him—that's all a
I'm going to say 'bout the little koala.

The Kiwi

The Kiwi's home is in a hole
A rabbit burrow serves her well
She digs the earth like any more
And my-oh-my! her egg is swell
It weighs well nigh a pound. My word!
An effort for a four pound bird!

Eee Yah! Hooray! She calls her spouse

That stupe comes running from the house
"Hop on that egg you knot head dunce
"An' hatch it out in just two months"
She smooths each separate feather out
And struts off to make walk-about.

So don't swap jobs with female birds
No matter how cantankerous
Stick to your own. Don't mess with hers
You'll find it really dangerous.

On Retirement

To all the good men who have done their best
To all the good friends who are seeking rest
I sing this song.
On the shadows are long with the rising sun
And the hummingbird's flight is clean and straight
And the track is plain where the deer has run
And the crow yells loud to his jet black mate
Oh the air is so clear I can reach the sky
And the mountains sit stodgily grimly there
Where the mallard drakes with their convoys fly
And the sweet smell of pine fires is light on the air
This is my song.
For who would be a slave to his work
When just for the taking these things are all his'n
For what price glory? What values lurk
In a cudgeled brain or a Pentagon prison
Oh this lad's finished his last report
And is thought with the study with blurry eyes
And this one's taken his last retort
From an empty head which will take his prize.
This is my song.
I wouldn't swap with any such swab
But where in hell can I find a job!

The Man in the Glass

When you get what you want in your struggle for self
And the world makes you king for a day
Just go to the mirror and look at yourself
And see what that man has to say.
For it isn't your father or mother or wife
Whose judgment upon you must pass.
The fellow whose verdict counts most in your life
Is the one staring back from the glass.

You may be like Jack Horner and chisel a plum
And think you're a wonderful guy.
The man in the glass says you're only a bum
If you can't look him straight in the eye.

He's the fellow to please—never mind all the rest,
For he's with you clean to the end.
And you've passed your most dangerous, difficult test
If the man in the glass is your friend.

You may fool the whole world down the pathway of years
And get pats on the back as you pass.
But your final reward will be heartache and tears
If you've cheated the man in the glass.

The small boy dug his toe in the sand

The small boy dug his toe in the sand
And looked far out on the created sea
"I have a treasure," his sober gaze
Full on my eyes as he turned to me.
"You can search forever through the lang
You can hunt clear down to the white sea sand
And you never will find it. It's mine alone
And I'll never share it with anyone."
Now what can it be? Please tell me why,
You think I can't find it if I should try.
"You'd miss it," he said,

"You'd hunt the and you'd search each grain
Of the white sea sand.
You'd look forever in distant coves.
And all the time it's here in my hand."
And the small boy grew and became a man
And search for treasure by land and sea.
But he found it not, though his eyes grew dim
And his hair grew gray as the ocean's foam
But he suddenly knew that his search was done.
He'd covered the sea and searched the world's land
And the treasure he sought was his own dear home
Which he'd always kept tight in his fisted hand.
And the song on his lips came straight from his heart.
And his journeys were ended, his harbor passed
For you were the treasure he held to fast.

Eulogium

We stood together—Cadets in the straining ranks
And visitors who sat in front, gazed at our immobility.
They little knew that in that gray-clad wall, dwelt laughter and
The love of life
The rightful boon to all our country's youth.

Nor did we know that Fate with steely pen had
Writ upon her book HERE STANDS A HERO
And this breast will bear the medals of his country's thanks
Wrought in the awful crucible of War.
And this one here, although a greater man, unknown
Shall lie in grave unmarked and indistinguishable
But all shall live forever to their friends.
And this, the next shall gasp our his young life
To gain a little time for leaders of a former day
To gather a great people for the fray.

And now their sons and grandsons, too,
Have marched along the Plain

And many in their turn have crossed that tree-clad river
Beyond which lies repose
To share their fathers' glory

And those of us who still remain to watch
Our thinning ranks grow thinner still
Feel deep within us well a silent prayer

O God, we ask compassion for our friends
Our prayers attend. For each of them
Gave of his best, his body heart and mind.
Each one we loved. Each sought a just reward
Receive him generously, we pray
Be kind, dear Lord.

Ancient Wisdom
by Harry J. Maloney

I want to tell you of of a dialogue I had with an old French peasant after we had side slipped into a cub landing field in Brittany upon my arrival from England in advance of my division.

My aide had gone to the single tent at the edge of the woods marking the landing field and I was sitting in the shade of a hedgerow smoking a cigarette waiting for him to return when a peasant with an ax on his shoulder, an old stained jacket and trousers, came shuffling along the road in his wooded shoes.

He glanced enviously at my cigarette and gave me *Bon jour*. I replied in French and offered him a cigarette. He accepted with thanks, I provided the match.

He said, "Well, M'sieur, the *Boches* have ruined France."

I asked him if he had been a soldier in World War I. Yes, he had. What branch? Infantry.

"Well," I said, "in 1914 when you were hurt much more than you have been in this war, you certainly didn't feel that the *Boche* had ruined France. Such talk would have been pretty harshly handled then."

He admitted that it was so. "Well then, how do you account for this change?"

The old man scratched his head. "You are right, General. We are in this fix now," he said, "because in 1914 when I was young, the youth asked, *What can we give to France?* Now, just prior to this war, we were all asking, *What can we get from France?* And so it was that the French nation has gone down and the *Boches* have ruined us."

In the light of what I saw later, I came to admire greatly the innate wisdom of the old man's statement.

Colonel Fatass

SOLDIER: [*Telephone rings.*] A Troop Orderly Room, whatdaya want!
VOICE: Soldier, you are slovenly and disrespectful. What would your Regimental Commander say if he heard you answer the telephone like that?
SOLDIER: You mean old Colonel Fatass.
VOICE: Do you know who this is?
SOLDIER: No, who is it?
VOICE: This is your Regimental Commander.
SOLDIER: Well do you know who this is?
VOICE: No.
SOLDIER: Well, so long Fatass.

Ancestors

Name	Year	Rank	Comments
James Barron	1804	Commodore U.S. Navy	Commodore was Highest Naval Rank. Campaign against Sultan of Morocco. Killed Stephen Decatur in a duel. My Great Great Uncle.
Samuel Lockett	Class 1854	Co. U.S. Corp of Engineers. Resign Commission for Confederacy. Col. Confederate Army Corps of Engineers	Married Daughter of Gov. Alabama. Constructed Fortifications, Mobile, Galveston, Vicksburg. Chief Engineer for Rulers of Egypt and Columbia. Signed Declaration of Loyalty after Civil War. Became Prof. Engineering at LSU. Supervised Raising of Statue of Liberty.
James Lockett	Class 1879	Col. U.S. Cavalry	Commanded 11th U.S. Cavalry in Southwest Indian Territory. Served in Moro Rebellion. Distinguished Service in Spanish & American War. Distinguished Service Medal.
James McDonald Lockett	Class 1908 (Did not grad.).		Served Philippine Scouts. Moro Campaign. INF. BN Commander (WWI). Wounded. Decorated Gallantry in Action. Commander Washington, D.C. district. Regimental commander. Commanded Infantry School, Fort Benning, Georgia.
Harry James Malony	1912	Maj. General (Ex-Artillery)	Served Panama during digging of canal. Served Texas-Mexican border. Served as Ordnance Officer and attached to French Airforce (WWI). Served as Secretary to Army Artillery School. Fort Sill Oklahoma. Artillery Board, Fort Bragg. Instructor Army War College. Chief U.S. negotiating committee with UK 1940–41. Headed Army War Plans. Commander 94th Inf. Div. U.S./Europe 1942–45. Heading negotiations and planning first Greek free elections (acted as Minister). Member UN Discussion Indochina. Member UN Discussion Philipines.
James Lockett Malony	Class 1945	Capt. Inf.	Infantry unit CMDR. Svd 7th U.S. Cav. Japan, Philippine Isles. BN-S-3 2nd Armored Div., Fort Sill, Oklahoma. Started own Consulting Company, Classified Clearances in U.S. Served various clients in UK, Russia, Spain, Germany, France, Italy. Liaison rulers of Nigeria, Liberia, Peru. Visibility Mideastern officials.

www.ingramcontent.com/pod-product-compliance
Lightning Source LLC
Chambersburg PA
CBHW020003050426
42450CB00005B/287